Fatemeh Fakhraie

Effects of Socioeconomic Status on Hijab Styles in Urban Iranian Women

Fatemeh Fakhraie

Effects of Socioeconomic Status on Hijab Styles in Urban Iranian Women

The role of education, social class, and income in Iranian women's hijab styles

VDM Verlag Dr. Müller

Impressum/Imprint (nur für Deutschland/ only for Germany)
Bibliografische Information der Deutschen Nationalbibliothek: Die Deutsche Nationalbibliothek verzeichnet diese Publikation in der Deutschen Nationalbibliografie; detaillierte bibliografische Daten sind im Internet über http://dnb.d-nb.de abrufbar.

Alle in diesem Buch genannten Marken und Produktnamen unterliegen warenzeichen-, marken- oder patentrechtlichem Schutz bzw. sind Warenzeichen oder eingetragene Warenzeichen der jeweiligen Inhaber. Die Wiedergabe von Marken, Produktnamen, Gebrauchsnamen, Handelsnamen, Warenbezeichnungen u.s.w. in diesem Werk berechtigt auch ohne besondere Kennzeichnung nicht zu der Annahme, dass solche Namen im Sinne der Warenzeichen- und Markenschutzgesetzgebung als frei zu betrachten wären und daher von jedermann benutzt werden dürften.

Coverbild: www.purestockx.com

Verlag: VDM Verlag Dr. Müller Aktiengesellschaft & Co. KG
Dudweiler Landstr. 99, 66123 Saarbrücken, Deutschland
Telefon +49 681 9100-698, Telefax +49 681 9100-988, Email: info@vdm-verlag.de
Zugl.: Corvallis, Oregon State University, Diss., 2008

Herstellung in Deutschland:
Schaltungsdienst Lange o.H.G., Berlin
Books on Demand GmbH, Norderstedt
Reha GmbH, Saarbrücken
Amazon Distribution GmbH, Leipzig
ISBN: 978-3-639-19104-2

Imprint (only for USA, GB)
Bibliographic information published by the Deutsche Nationalbibliothek: The Deutsche Nationalbibliothek lists this publication in the Deutsche Nationalbibliografie; detailed bibliographic data are available in the Internet at http://dnb.d-nb.de .
Any brand names and product names mentioned in this book are subject to trademark, brand or patent protection and are trademarks or registered trademarks of their respective holders. The use of brand names, product names, common names, trade names, product descriptions etc. even without a particular marking in this works is in no way to be construed to mean that such names may be regarded as unrestricted in respect of trademark and brand protection legislation and could thus be used by anyone.

Cover image: www.purestockx.com

Publisher:
VDM Verlag Dr. Müller Aktiengesellschaft & Co. KG
Dudweiler Landstr. 99, 66123 Saarbrücken, Germany
Phone +49 681 9100-698, Fax +49 681 9100-988, Email: info@vdm-publishing.com

Copyright © 2009 by the author and VDM Verlag Dr. Müller Aktiengesellschaft & Co. KG and licensors
All rights reserved. Saarbrücken 2009

Printed in the U.S.A.
Printed in the U.K. by (see last page)
ISBN: 978-3-639-19104-2

ACKNOWLEDGEMENTS

I express sincere appreciation to my parents, my friends, and my colleagues in Oregon State University who helped me brainstorm, translate, and edit this manuscript.

Special thanks go to Dr. Kathy Mullet, Mehra, Baba, and Najmeh for their help with my survey and translations.

TABLE OF CONTENTS

	Page
CHAPTER ONE: INTRODUCTION	1
Purpose of study	1
Hypothesis	2
Assumptions	2
Limitations	3
Definition of Terms	4
Historical Background	5
CHAPTER TWO: REVIEW OF LITERATURE	17
Introduction	17
Socioeconomic Status as Determinant of Attitudes	18
Hijab	19
Socioeconomic Demography in Iran	21
Conclusion	22
CHAPTER THREE: METHODS	23
Development of Instrument	23
Sample Selection	25
Data Collection	26
Advantages and Disadvantages of Online Surveys	27
Data Analysis	28

TABLE OF CONTENTS (Continued)

                                                                Page

CHAPTER FOUR: RESULTS..29

    Survey Results...29

    Data Summary...44

    Research Objectives and Hypothesis.........................45

    Post-Hoc Tests...56

CHAPTER FIVE: SUMMARY AND CONCLUSIONS............59

    Summary..59

    Research Objectives and Hypothesis Conclusions..........60

    Limitations...62

    Recommendations...63

    Recommendations for Further Study.........................63

    Implications of This Study......................................64

BIBLIOGRAPHY..65

APPENDICES..69

    Appendix A: Informed Consent................................70

    Appendix B: Survey...72

    Appendix C: Email Message...................................84

    Appendix D: Figures of Iranian *Hijab* Styles................86

LIST OF TABLES

Table	Page
1. Source of fashion knowledge	30
2. Style of hijab worn out with friends	31
3. Rankings of cost, trendiness, modesty, and comfort in potential clothes to wear out with friends	31
4. Importance of brand names	32
5. Importance of color-coordination in outfits	32
6. Color preference in outfits	33
7. Embellishment preference	33
8. Word expressing style preference	34
9. Age of respondent	37
10. Marital status of respondent	37
11. Health insurance of respondent	38
12. Respondent's internet sources	38
13. Respondent's housemate status	39
14. Respondent's level of education	39
15. Respondent's employment status	40
16. Respondent's monthly income	40
17. Education level of respondent's mother	41
18. Education level of respondent's father	41
19. Education level of respondent's spouse	42
20. Employment status of respondent's mother	42
21. Employment status of respondent's father	43

LIST OF TABLES (Continued)

Table	Page
22. Employment status of respondent's spouse	43
23. Monthly household income of respondent's parents	44
24. Monthly income of respondent's spouse	44
25. Correlation of outerwear style with fashion preference variable	46
26. Chi-squared of hijab preference and cost importance	51
27. Chi-squared of modesty and education variables	51
28. Chi-squared of modesty and income variables	52
29. Chi-squared of mother's education and brand importance	53
30. Chi-squared of mother's education and preference for dark colors	54
31. Chi-squared of father's education and preference for dark colors	54
32. Chi-squared of father's education and preference for light clothing	55
33. Chi-squared of parent's income and preference for light colors	56
34. Correlation between marital and fashion preference variables	57
35. Chi-squared test of marital status and preference for dark colors	58

CHAPTER I

INTRODUCTION

For the past several decades, U.S. relations with the Islamic Republic of Iran (IRI) have been tense, and many Americans are misinformed or completely uninformed about the IRI and its people. One of the main sources of confusion is *hijab,* clothing which conceals a woman's hair and bodily curves. The IRI mandates that all women wear *hijab*. The Iranian *hijab* is often confused with other regional styles of *hijabs*, which leads to a monolithic representation of *hijab* in the West.

Also, my personal experience with and research on Iranian women illustrates that different styles of *hijab* indicate origin from different cities or regions of the country and levels of religious observance. This idea led me to research the socioeconomic influences on women's *hijab* styles within the IRI in order to try and illustrate multidimensionality within both *hijabs* and Iranians. There are many differing styles of *hijab*, and I argue that socioeconomic status influences the different styles that young women choose.

Purpose of Study

The purpose of this study is to determine whether socioeconomic status correlates with *hijab* style preferences in a public social setting (i.e., out with friends, out shopping, etc.). This research focuses on the relationship between certain socio-economic indicators and *hijab* style preferences in Iranian women. Specifically, I want to determine if socio-economic indicators of respondents' education and income, parents' educations and incomes, correlate with *hijab* style preferences of young (ages 15-30) urban Iranian women.

I focus on urban women because urban women are much more likely to have different sources of internet access (i.e., an internet café, university access, home access, etc.) and thus would be more likely to complete a web-based survey, while rural women are not. Thus, I exclude rural women from my study. Also, I concentrate on the 15-30 age group because this age group has grown up with the mandatory observation of Islamic clothing in their everyday life; I want to concentrate on women who have practiced mandatory *hijab* their entire life so the *hijab* is seen as a part of everyday life rather than an issue of contention.

My objectives are:

1. To determine the socioeconomic status of 15-30 year old urban Iranian women
2. To determine what *hijab* styles young urban Iranian women prefer in a public social setting
3. To determine if there are correlations between these socioeconomic indicators and *hijab* style preference

Hypothesis

Young, urban Iranian women's preferences (those in the 15 – 30 age group) regarding *hijab* styles will reflect their socioeconomic status.

Assumptions

For this study, I make the assumption that:

1. All respondents are literate in Farsi.
2. Socioeconomic status is determined by father's, mother's, and respondent's incomes and education levels, as well as things like health care and internet access (Lewis et al, 1985; Mehryar & Tashakkori, 1984; Mehryar & Tashakkori, 1978).
3. *Hijab* styles indicate differences in socioeconomic status.

Limitations

The limitations of this study are:

1. I will be conducting this survey using a web-based survey.
2. My study will exclude rural women because there is limited or no access to internet in smaller rural areas.
3. My study may unintentionally exclude uneducated or low-income women who do not have access to university or personal computers/internet service/connection.
4. As participation will be through self-selection, my responses may be confined to those who are interested in fashion.
5. My research focuses on the clothing that women wear in public, so I will not be able to get an accurate picture of their private style preferences.
6. Because of recent fines and arrests made in conjunction with *hijab* preferences, my respondents may suspect my intentions or identity, which could affect their participation.

7. My respondents may be afraid of internet monitoring by the Iranian government, and thus may not respond accurately.
8. I will have difficulty building rapport with my subjects because this is an impersonal and remote survey; however, this may work to my advantage if the respondents feel that they can answer anonymously.

Despite these limitations, this study will provide data on the style preferences of urban Iranian women. This study will provide insight on how young, urban Iranian women conform to governmental dress codes while expressing themselves through their dress, and will hopefully begin to fill in an empty void of knowledge about Middle Eastern women's connections to fashion.

Definition of Terms

Ahadith- Reports on the sayings and traditions of the Prophet Mohammad. Also referred to as the *sunna*.

Ayatollah- A high ranking title given to Shi'a clerics who are experts in Islamic studies such as jurisprudence, ethics, and philosophy.

Caliph- (also spelled Khalifah). Refers to a representative or a successor to the Prophet Mohammad.

Chador- *Chador* is a form of *hijab*, consisting of a full-length semi-circular piece of material that is placed on top of the head and covers the entire body. It is usually held in place with the hands. See Figure 1 in Appendix D.

Hijab- Islamic clothing that covers a woman's hair and her bodily curves. The *hijab* may also cover ears, neck, and the bosom. For this study, we will use the word *hijab* to denote the head covering *and* the body covering. The types of *hijab* we look at in this study are: chador, maghnaeh, and roosari. See Figures 1, 2, and 3 in Appendix D.

Imam- A religious leader, or anyone who leads a congregational prayer. In Shi'a Islam, Imams are considered similar to Catholic priests: they play an active role in the local community and often times in the government.

The Holy Qur'an- The holy book of the Muslim faith. Muslims believe that this is the literal word of Allah (God).

Magnaeh- A pull-on style of *hijab* that is usually worn as part of a uniform, such as in the workplace or university setting. See Figure 2 in Appendix D.

Roosari- A loose headscarf style of *hijab*. See Figure 3 in Appendix D.

Shah- A Persian title meaning "king" or "emperor."

Shari'a- Islamic law. Shari'a consists of legislation within the scope and dimensions of the Qur'an.

Sura- Designates a chapter in the Holy Qur'an.

'Ulama- A body of educated scholars who have the authority to give a ruling on questions related to Islamic law (shari'a) and theology.

Historical Background

The histories of Islam, Iran, and Islam *in* Iran are long and complicated, but are imperative for the reader's understanding of the culture and religion discussed in this thesis. This section will outline these histories as succinctly as possible.

Islam

Islam is the faith of the Muslims. Islam follows in the Abrahamic tradition of both Judaism and Christianity, and incorporates many of their teachings and prophets in its holy book, The Holy Qur'an. Muslims see the Holy Qur'an as the literal word of Allah.

The two main branches of Islam are Sunni and Shi'a. Shi'a is the branch of Islam that the Islamic Republic of Iran adheres to; the Shi'a branch also has a significant majority in Iraq and Lebanon.

At the core of the difference between Shi'a and Sunni belief is Islamic history. The Shi'a believe that Ali, the Prophet's son-in-law, should have succeeded the Prophet after his death because they believe the Prophet designated Ali to be his successor; in short, the caliphate is inherited. The Sunni believe that the caliphate is appointed, not inherited (Berkey, 2003).

Another issue is that the Shi'a believe that Allah provides each generation with an Imam, who is the rightful leader of the community, whereas the Sunni believe that Islamic law and mores are brought about by the Islamic scholars' (the *ulama*) consensus. In Shi'a Islam, the Imam is determined by designation from a predecessor, just as the Prophet had designated Ali as his successor (Berkey, 2003). This is a rejection of the Sunni belief that the caliphate is appointed, not inherited.

The Shi'a and the Sunni parted into factions and have vied for political control for centuries. Sunnis set up dynasties and caliphs and expected the Shi'a to adhere to these rulers. The Shi'a resisted these rulers, often militarily, and set up their own rulers and caliphs during the centuries after the Prophet's death.

By the tenth century, the Twelver sect of the Shi'a had finalized a place for itself in the Shi'a scene. Twelver Shi'ism is a sect which believes in the infallibility in twelve major Imams who came after the Prophet. These Imams were members of the Prophet's family and are recognized as rightful leaders. The line of Imams begins with Ali, the Prophet's son-in-law, and ends with Muhammad al-Mahdi, the last in the line of Imam descendents. Al-Mahdi is a messianic figure in Shi'a Islam: according to Shi'a belief, he has been in hiding since the ninth century, and will return at the end of time to reveal Allah's plan for humanity (Berkey, 2003; Momen, 1985; Keddie, 1980).

Both the Shi'a and the Sunni accept the Holy Qu'ran as the word of Allah. Different Shi'a and Sunni sects accept different parts of the ahadith differently, but a majority of Muslims accept the ahadith as the sayings of the Prophet Muhammad that answer any questions not answered by the Holy Qur'an.

A majority of Muslims also see the *hijab* as mandated by Allah. However, the term "hijab" is *never* used in the context of a woman's clothing in the Holy Qur'an (El Guindi, 1999). *Sura al-Noor* 24:31 is the one *sura* (passage) which most people point to for an illustration of the requirement of *hijab*. This passage states that women should dress modestly and should not reveal themselves to men outside their family.

Including the *sura* here is problematic because of the translations. Many Islamic scholars translate differently, and there are Islamic scholars who feel that *hijab* is *not* mandated by the Holy Qur'an. Different translation in English will use different words. For example, here are two different translations of the same passage:

> [24:31] And tell the believing women to subdue their eyes, and maintain their chastity. They shall not reveal any parts of their bodies, except that which is necessary. They shall cover their chests, and shall not relax this code in the presence of other than their husbands, their fathers, the fathers of their

> husbands, their sons, the sons of their husbands, their brothers, the sons of their brothers, the sons of their sisters, other women, the male servants or employees whose sexual drive has been nullified, or the children who have not reached puberty. They shall not strike their feet when they walk in order to shake and reveal certain details of their bodies. All of you shall repent to GOD, O you believers, that you may succeed.

This is taken from http://submission.org, which is an authorized English translation of the Holy Qur'an online (2007). But it does not mention the *hijab* or the veil for women at all, and commands women simply to dress modestly and "cover their chests". This next version, taken from a Yusuf Ali translation (2001), uses the word veil:

> And say to the believing women that they should lower their gaze and guard their modesty; that they should not display their beauty and ornaments except what (must ordinarily) appear thereof; that they should draw their veils over their bosoms and not display their beauty except to their husbands, their fathers, their husband's fathers, their sons, their husbands' sons, their brothers or their brothers' sons, or their sisters' sons, or their women, or the slaves whom their right hands possess, or male servants free of physical needs, or small children who have no sense of the shame of sex; and that they should not strike their feet in order to draw attention to their hidden ornaments. And O ye Believers! turn ye all together towards Allah, that ye may attain Bliss.

Many Muslims believe this verse commands women to wear *hijab*, but there are many other Muslims and Islamic scholars who believe that these verses say only to dress modesty, not to cover their hair.

Iran

Iran is nearly three millennia old (Kamiar, 2007a). Ancient Greeks referred to Iran as "Persia," and for the next several centuries, the world followed suit. Even until the early twentieth century, the rest of the world mistakenly knew Iran as "Persia". In

1935, Reza Shah, the ruler of Iran at the time, asked the world to call Iran by its proper, indigenous name instead of Persia (Kamiar, 2007a; Yarshater, 1989).

Iran has a long history, and most of that history has been ruled over by dynasties. Ruling dynasties were in place earlier than ancient Greek historians could document them: Herodotus and Xenophon acknowledged that Iran's Achaemenid Dynasty (559-330 BCE) founded a federal state, a vast commonwealth of autonomous nations in the 5th century BCE (Mojtahed-Zadeh, 2007). Nashat (2003) states that although pre-Achaemenid Iran did not require women to veil themselves, veiling was probably introduced after the conquest of Greek and Assyrian territories (whose cultures mandated seclusion and veiling).

From this era all the way up until the twentieth century, Iran's borders expanded with conquests by the Persian state and shrank in accordance with conquests, first by Romans, then by Arabs from the Arabian Peninsula, then by the Seljuq Turks from Central Asia, then by Mongolians in East Asia. Iran's political control had once been from Egypt all the way to India and Uzbekistan. Under many conquerors, Iran's borders were expanded or lost, and Iranian political control slowly shrunk to the size that we now know it.

The first conquerors that helped shape what Iran is today are the Arabs. The fall of the Persian Empire was a result of the Caliph Umar's conquest of Iran in the seventh century, a few years after Prophet Muhammad died. Though Iran quickly fell, the majority of Iranians did not convert to Islam immediately; this will be discussed in the "Islam in Iran" section. Though Muslims now ran the country and put in place certain rules for Muslims and non-Muslims alike, Iranians' influence on their conquers and resistance to Arab acculturation was highlighted in the adoption of certain cloth, clothing colors, and diets by Arabs in Iran (Choksy, 2003). Women's roles in the newly-Islamic Iran changed little: wealthy women still could assert their economic power; poorer women were still sold as slaves or maids (Choksy, 2003).

The conquests of the Turks and Mongolians (in the tenth century and the thirteenth century, respectively) brought little more than dynastic in-fighting, the erratic expanding and reducing of Iranian borders, and rulers who cared little for the Iranian people (Kamiar, 2007b; Morgan, 1988). Women were used for economic and political alliances in both these periods as well: "Their domain was the home, their responsibilities were domestic and familial, and their lifestyle was circumscribed by Islamic social norms" (Hillenbrand, 2003; p. 116). Paintings from the Seljuq Turk period indicates that women did not veil themselves at court, perhaps in line with their Turkic traditions (Hillenbrand, 2003). Royal women also could influence politics and manipulate rulers (their husbands or their sons, in most cases) (Hillenbrand, 2003; Forbes Manz, 2003).

The next dynasty that helped shape Iran into its modern-day equivalent was the Safavid dynasty. The most important figure in the Safavid dynasty was Shah Isma'il I, who contributed to the founding of many segments of Iran's current borders and establishing Shi'ism in Iran, to be discussed in the section "Islam in Iran." Shah Abbas I, another Safavid figure, expanded trade with the English and Dutch East India Companies, and established European tourism within Iran (Morgan, 1988). In Safavid Iran, women veiled, but women of importance wore a face veil so that only their eyes showed; women of low status wore headscarves but let their faces and bosoms show.

(Szuppe, 2003). Many women were used for political and economic alliances, just as in previous dynasties. Many women important in dynastic politics fought in military campaigns, had their own courts, and directed royal politics (Szuppe, 2003).

After the Afsharid and Zand dynasties, which were relatively peaceful and short but not modernizing, the Qajar dynasty came to power. According to author David Morgan: "If there is a dividing line between the 'medieval' and the 'modern' history of [Iran], …it is at the beginning of the Qājār dynasty" (1988; p. 158).

The Qajar dynasty lasted from 1794 to 1945, and saw an unprecedented amount of interaction with the West. Previously, the Muslim world had been the center of military power and scientific knowledge; the Industrial revolution created a surge of military power for the West, which resulted in military defeats for the Muslim world. As a result of these losses, the Muslim world acknowledged the new military prowess of the West and used western education to gain this knowledge (Mahdavi, 2004). Iranian students were sent to the West and Europeans came to Iran for diplomacy, vacation, or employment in the western-style universities that the shah was building.

Education was not the only contact with Westerners. Russia invaded Iran twice during the Qajar era and Iran signed economic treaties with both Britain and the U.S. (Kamiar, 2007b). Westernization slowly permeated the upper classes; Nasir al-Din Shah's daughter, Princess Taj al-Saltana, was so swayed by her European education that she rejected Iranian customs and started wearing western clothes, going bareheaded, and drinking wine (Mahdavi, 2004).

The women of the Qajar era were viewed as subordinate: according to an 1891 treatise for women named *Dar bayan-I ta'dib al-nisvan* (Statement concerning the proper upbringing of women), "the family is an important unit in which the father is the all-powerful patriarch and the wife and children are obedient servants" (Mahdavi, 2004). However, education and class frequently played a part in how obedient women were: upper class women frequently divorced or married whom they pleased, even though Fath Ali Shah used his children's marriages to improve ties with enemies. Many lower-class women used marriages with the shahs to improve their status and influence (Nashat, 2004b). Many middle-class women were literate and used their education to influence their husband's affairs, become religious mystics, or open schools for girls (Mahdavi, 2004).

The Qajar era came to an end in 1925, when Reza Khan toppled the Qajars though a military coup d'etat and established the Pahlavi dynasty, crowning himself as Reza Shah Pahlavi. The most tumultuous modernization policies and western influences happened during this time, and the position of women changed dramatically. Reza Shah aimed to introduce western-style practices and institutions to Iran: he opened the first public school for girls and ensured that women attended the newly-formed Tehran University (Nashat, 2004a). He also outlawed the veil and decreed that women were to be bareheaded or their veils would be taken off by police. This benefited upper-class and educated women, but the middle- and lower-classes in smaller towns resisted (Nashat, 2004a, Hoodfar, 1997; Ahmed, 1992).

Iran was brought into World War II by the invasions of the U.S.S.R. and Britain, despite Iran's neutrality. Reza Shah was deposed and sent into exile by an

Anglo-Soviet decision, and his son, Mohammed Reza Shah, was crowned in 1941 (Mojtahed-Zadeh, 2007; Kamiar, 2007b). Only a decade later, Dr. Mohammed Mossadeq, who headed the Marxist party of Iran, was elected prime minister. He was prime minister for three years, but was forcefully removed by the shah, with the help of the U.S. and the U.K., for his nationalist agitations and his attempt to nationalize the oil industry (Mojtahed-Zadeh, 2007; Kamiar, 2007b). After Mossadeq's removal, the shah enfranchised women, enacted laws which gave women more rights in family law, and reformed land ownership. But these reforms did not improve the lives of lower- and middle-class Iranians, many of whom demonstrated against the shah. Many middle-class women who did not normally wear a veil would take up the *chador* (see Figure 1 in Appendix D) for demonstrations against the Shah. They and others demonstrated their dissatisfaction and resistance to forced Westernization by the Shah's regime (El Guindi, 1999; Hoodfar, 1997; Betteridge, 1983).

Demonstrations led to a coup in which Mohammed Reza Shah was deposed and exiled, and the previously-exiled Ayatollah Khomeini returned to Iran to assume leadership of a new Islamic state that his supporters had demonstrated for. On April 1, 1979, Iran became an Islamic republic (Kamiar, 2007b), which meant that Islamic law *(shari'a)* was now political law, and that Ayatollah Khomeini was the Supreme Leader of the country. The government repealed all of the political protections for women and suggested that women emulate more traditional, Islamic role models and take up Islamic clothing instead of wearing Western clothes; Islamic clothing became mandatory in 1980 (Nashat, 2004a).

Iraq invaded Iran in 1980 in a war that lasted until 1988. Women filled the workplace, taking the empty places of men who were fighting against Iraq (Nashat, 2004a). During this time, the Reagan administration sold arms to Iran despite the fact that Iran-U.S. ties had been broken since the Islamic Revolution. This was known as the Iran-Contra affair (Kamiar, 2007b).

Ayatollah Khomeini died in 1989, and another Supreme Leader, Ayatollah Khamenei, is appointed (Kamiar, 2007b). Despite Ayatollah Khamenei's lack of endorsement, Mohammad Khatami was elected President of Iran in 1997 on a reformist platform. Khatami was reelected in 2001(Kamiar, 2007b; Nashat, 2004a). In 2005, Mahmoud Ahmedinejad was elected on an anti-corruption platform. Conservatives had gained control of parliament a year before he was elected (Kamiar, 2007b).

Today, the position of women in Iran is still dictated by Islamic political and social mores: every summer there are waves of arrests for women who don't dress "Islamically" enough. But women are an increasing presence in the universities and workplaces, and women continue to make spaces for themselves both in Iran and out: Shirin Ebadi won Iran's first Nobel Prize in 2003 for her work promoting women's and children's rights in Iran (Kamiar, 2007b; Nashat, 2004a).

Islam in Iran

As stated earlier, Islam came to Iran with the Islamic conquest of Caliph Umar in the seventh century. The caliph brought Sunni Islam to Iran, and the country remained predominately Sunni for the next eight centuries. However, Iranians didn't automatically convert as soon as the Muslims came into power; the majority of conversions happened between the eighth and thirteenth centuries (Choksy, 2003).

When Shah Ismail came to power in 1501, the majority of the population was still Sunni. The shah made Shi'ism the official religion of Iran and made conversion to Twelver Shi'ism compulsory (Morgan, 1988; Keddie, 1980). Currently, Twelver Shi'ism is still Iran's official religion: over 90 percent of Iran's Muslims are Shi'a (Keddie, 1980). The remaining Muslims are Sunni or from other Islamic sects, and Iran still has a small number of Jews, Baha'is, and Zoroastrians.

Since 1979, Iran has been a theocratic republic. The beginning of influence by the *'ulama* on the government can be traced to Qajar-era Iran, so the idea of an Iran controlled by Islamic clerics is not entirely new (Keddie, 1980). However, in 1979, the Islamic Revolution set up a government entirely headed by the *'ulama*, which changed Iran inside and out. The head of the country was now the Supreme Leader, Ayatollah Khomeini, and subsequent rulers would also be ayatollahs. The country has a president and a parliament that is elected into office by the people; however, the final say on all matters of state *and* religion are made by the Supreme Leader.

This theocratic government ensured that *shari'a* (Islamic law) was the official legislative code for the country; any existing laws contradicting *shari'a* were repealed, and no laws proposed are allowed to contradict *shari'a*. As stated earlier, the government also made that *hijab* mandatory for every woman in the country, Iranian or foreign, and enforced this policy.

Despite the bleak representation of an Islamic Republic seen in the West, women in the IRI continue to live their lives how they see fit. Women see the *hijab* in different ways, but most have come to accept its place in their life and country; these women work, marry, raise children, and go to school, without letting the issue of *hijab* get in their way.

CHAPTER II

REVIEW OF LITERATURE

Introduction

The oldest and most agreed-upon theory of fashion is the "social differentiation" theory: that one of fashion's main functions is to convey the social and economic status of its wearer (Lurie, 1981; Simmel, 1971; Veblen, 1912). It is generally agreed that individual values, interests and attitudes are related to clothing behavior and clothing choices (Ryan, 1966). Applying these theories to young, urban Iranian women constructs my hypothesis (whether socioeconomic status will influence *hijab* style preferences).

However, no studies have revealed how an individual's clothing style choices manifest themselves when the clothing is mandated by the government. Currently, there is an exceedingly small amount of literature that describes the *hijab* as fashion, or how socio-economic status may indicate fashion preferences in *hijab* styles; most research describes different types of *hijab* as only regional or religious indicators. My project deals with compulsory *hijab*; in Iran, there is no question if one will wear *hijab*—it is mandatory. Including a debate on whether women should wear *hijab* or not is beyond the scope of my project. Thus, I am interested in seeing of the "social differentiation" theory is applicable to young, urban Iranian women.

In the literature review, socio-economic status as a determinant of attitudes in Iran and a truncated exploration of the symbolism of the Islamic *hijab* is explored. The review is structured into sections. The socio-economic status as determinant of attitudes passage will be organized through parents' and respondent's education as a variable. The section on *hijab* will define *hijab* and reasons that it is worn, then will follow the use of the *hijab* for cultural, political and gender symbols. To provide a background and benchmark for this study, a review of the current socioeconomic status of Iranian households will be reported.

Socioeconomic Status as Determinant of Attitudes

Discretionary income, as demonstrated by Lewis, Dyer, & Moran (1985), is a strong factor on young women's spending on clothes. This indicates that the more discretionary income a young woman has (as tied to her socioeconomic status: the higher her socioeconomic status, the more discretionary income she has), the more she might spend on clothes. Fung and Yuen (2002) reported that female youth in Hong Kong with a higher socioeconomic status were more interested in their clothing than their counterparts with lower socioeconomic statuses.

Parents' education is a significant indicator of a youth's socio-economic status in Iran (Mehryar & Tashakkori, 1978; Mehryar & Tashakkori, 1984). Education is similarly important for the respondents themselves. After the Revolution, education became more comprehensive and accessible for Iranian women, and women currently make up approximately 60 percent of total university graduates (Shaditalab, 2005). Many Iranian women go to college in hopes of increasing their value in the "marriage market" (i.e., find a husband who has a higher education level and a higher-paying job) or to try for financial independence through the labor market (Shavarini, 2006; Shavarini, 2005). Shavarini, in her 2006 study on the influence of higher education on

Iranian women's lives, indicates that many Iranian women who attend college express themselves through their *hijab* styles and makeup.

Hijab

Many Muslims believe that hijab is obligatory for Muslim women. However, "hijab" is not the Arabic word for "veil," despite the fact that many authors use the word "*hijab*" interchangeably with "veil" or "headscarf." Some authors, however, use *hijab* as a more inclusive term of Islamic clothing, which includes covering the hair, neck, bosom, and womanly curves (El Guindi, 2005; El Guindi, 1999). The majority of the authors in my review use "*hijab*" and "veil" as synonymous. In most of the articles I read, *hijab* was either defined as a head scarf or not defined at all.

For this study, the definition of *hijab* will include both headscarf and/or clothes that cover the body.

Chico (2000) asserts that the Islamic *hijab* is worn for sexual modesty and the social separation of women. These reasons mirror the use of the modern *hijab* as a way to identify with Islamic movements or identities (Hessini, 1994). Haddad (1984) states that Muslim women may wear the *hijab* for several different reasons. She names nine:

- religious (as a symbol of religious commitment or submission to God's will)
- economic (as a sign of wealth)
- practical (as a way to reduce clothing costs)
- demographic (as an indicator of urban dwellers)

- cultural (as a public statement of morality)
- domestic (as compliance with family members' wishes)
- psychological (as a symbol of cultural or Islamic authenticity)
- political (as a symbol of defiance against or conformity with political ideology/group)
- revolutionary (as a symbol of the need for an Islamic society).

These reasons are not completely exhaustive or exclusive: "revolutionary" reasons could easily fall under the "political" category, her description of "practical" could easily be included in the "economic" category, and her description of "economic" reasons is more compatible with the idea of *hijab* as an indicator of status, as it was in pre-Islamic times (Nashat, 2003; El Guindi, 1999; Ahmed, 1992). Also, her "demographic" category leaves out the idea of *hijab* as an indicator of which region or country a Muslim woman is from, which *hijab* styles often communicate. Her "cultural" and "psychological" reasons sound similar, and her categories exclude the ideas of *hijab* as a protector from non-kin males, or as a diffuser of beauty. These two reasons often play a significant part of why women wear *hijab* (Ali, 2005; Cole & Ahmadi, 2003; Eid, 2002; Seikaly, 1998; Hoodfar, 1997; Hessini, 1994). All these contradictions or omissions result in my disposal of Haddad's reasons to outline my review of literature on the *hijab*.

When dealing with the idea of Islamic clothing as fashionable, Moors (2007) points to women of San'a, Yemen, and illustrates how differing styles of Islamic clothing serve as different indicators of social status and fashion, while Osella & Osella (2007) point to different styles of Islamic dress in South India as indicators of different social statuses. Balasescu (2007) introduces us to two Iranian designers who cater to upper-class clientele and examines fashion photography in a culture that aims to downplay the female form.

Socioeconomic Demography in Iran

According to the Statistical Centre of Iran (2001), 66 percent of Iran's population is settled in urban areas and 22 percent of Iran's population is of the 15-24 age group. This same report tells us that the median age for Iranian women is 20.7 and the mean age for women is 25.6. The mean age of first marriage is 23.4 for women.

As for Iranian women's workforce participation, the report (2001) tells us that women (aged 15 and over) participate in economic activity only 14 percent, compared to men's participation at 77.3 percent. Looking at unemployment figures, 17.8 percent of women aged 15 and over are unemployed, compared to 13.7 percent for men. These figures seem to contradict figures given by Shaditalab (2005), which state that 60 percent of university students are women. Shaditalab explains that, because of patriarchal institutions and Iran's traditional view of men as the breadwinners, female employment continues to be low because women are not being hired at the same rate as men.

Looking at currency, the exchange rate for the Iranian *rial* to the U.S. dollar on October 15, 2007 was: 9,328.0 rials per 1 dollar (Yahoo! Finance). In the Household Income-Expenditure Project of the Statistical Centre of Iran (2000a), the statistics divided urban households into five income categories: 7,200,000 rials and lower per month (approx. $771.87); 7,200,001 - 9,000,000 rials per month (approx. $771.87 - $964.84); 9,000,001-12,000,000 rials per month (approx. $964.84 - $1,286.45);

12,000,001 -19,500,000 per month (approx. $1,286.45 - $2,090.45); and 19,500,000 rials and over.

Despite these categories, this same study indicated that the average household expenditure per month is 2,014,583.00 rials (approximately $221.94). Thus, we can assume that the average Iranian salary is somewhere around 2,000,000 rials, which falls into the lowest income bracket.

Conclusion

Based on the basic clothing theory (Lurie, 1981; Simmel, 1971; Veblen, 1912) that clothing preferences represent the socio-economic level of the wearer, my literature review looked at the socioeconomic demography of Iranians and Iranian women, how socioeconomic status can determine attitudes, and the definition of *hijab* and how it serves as an indicator of fashion wearer.

Several of the articles I used in my literature review, particularly those of the socioeconomic status indicators, directly influenced my methods: I used them to inform my survey and compile my sample. The articles show that *hijab* comes in different styles that may connote different social statuses.

CHAPTER III

METHODS

The purpose of this study is to determine the correlation between the socioeconomic status of young urban Iranian women and their *hijab* style preferences. A web survey was used to ascertain the socioeconomic status of these women and which *hijab* styles they prefer. The *hijab* is required to be worn by all women in Iran and therefore the particular style worn by a woman may be an indication of her socioeconomic status. I used the referral method to obtain the sample for this study. This method has limitations in the possible sample size which might be obtained, but provides the best method of data collection for the researcher because of time, monetary, and geographical restraints.

Development of Instrument

The purpose of using an online survey is to determine a link between young urban Iranian women's socioeconomic status and their clothing preferences when I am not in the same physical location as my respondents. I developed my own survey, as there was a lack of similar studies in the field. An original questionnaire was developed to collect data on each research objective (Appendix A). The review of literature, informal conversations with Iranians, and the researcher's personal experience shaped the basis for the survey.

The questions developed collect data in two areas: socioeconomic status and personal *hijab* style preference. For the first objective, certain questions about education, income, and family help the researcher ascertain the respondents' socioeconomic status. For the second objective, the first section of the questionnaire uses behavioral questions to determine the style preferences of the respondents.

When discussing income, I elaborated upon the five salary categories set by the Statistical Centre of Iran (2000) to get a better idea of the economic boundaries of the lowest economic group. For my survey, I divided these five categories into eight:

- 500,000 rials or less ($53.49 or less per month)
- 500,001 – 1,000,000 rials ($53.49 -$106.97 per month)
- 1,000,001 – 5,000,000 rials ($106.97 - $534.87 per month)
- 5,000,000 -- 7,200,000 rials ($534.87 - $770.22 per month)
- 7,200,001 -- 9,000,000 rials ($770.22 - $962.77 per month)
- 9,000,001 – 12,000,000 rials ($962.77 - $1,283.70 per month)
- 12,000,001 – 19,500,000 rials ($1,283.70 – $2,086.01 per month)
- 19,500,000 rials or more ($2,086.01 or more per month)

For my data analysis, I re-classified these groups as low, middle, and high incomes. The low income group included respondents from 500,000 rials or less to 7,200,000 rials per month. The middle income group included respondents from 7,200,001 rials to 12,000,000 rials per month. The high income group included 12,000,001 to 19,500,000 rials or more per month.

I developed a questionnaire in English and sent it to two Iranian contacts (family members), who then translated the survey into Farsi. The contacts are fluent in both Farsi and English. I then sent one contact's translation to other, and had these contacts translate the survey back into English to ensure the Farsi questions mirrored the English ones. The Farsi version of the questionnaire was used for the on-line survey (Appendix B).

I developed the pretest of this survey in an earlier Oregon State University course, and tested on members from the *Yahoo! Groups* "utcom81_Girls" group. This group consists of 34 members, all of whom are young women living in Tehran, Iran. I was introduced to the group by my cousin, who is also in the group. Approximately 13 responses were received. Since the questionnaire was only in English, the only respondents were upper-class, Western-educated Iranians. Findings from the pilot suggested that having the survey in Farsi would be more effective at appealing to a broader sample, and that the majority of respondents focused on *hijab* as fashion.

Sample Selection

Referral method (sometimes referred to as "snowball sampling" or "respondent-driven sampling") is what Welch (1975) describes as "When one member of the target population is located, he or she is asked to name other members of the target population, who are then interviewed and asked to supply additional names, and so forth" (pp. 238). Welch points to the method's defects as bias through under-sampling of isolated community members and over-sampling of community members with "more extensive contacts and acquaintances," which can lead to biases in socioeconomic status and an omission of "those whose views may be unpopular within the community." Welch suggests that bias can be minimized through inclusion: the more respondents, the less bias possible, though isolation of some demographics may still occur.

In order to minimize bias, I have narrowed my demographic categories to be as specific as possible so that my data doesn't claim to speak for more people than it really does. I presented the introduction and survey in Farsi to facilitate non-English speakers' participation in the study.

I have five close personal contacts (all family members) in Iran to whom I sent the survey. The *Yahoo! Group* "utcom81_Girls" has approximately 34 members who were potential participants in the study. By asking each of these contacts to refer the survey to 10 more friends using the referral method of sampling, a possible sample size of 390 may be obtained.

Data Collection

I sent the survey through links via email to personal contacts in Iran and posted in a Yahoo! Group boards for the group "utcom81_Girls". The emails included:

1. a short message asking for their help in completing the survey and a request that they forward the email to ten of their female friends
2. an informed consent document explaining the purpose of the research, the risks and benefits to the respondent
3. a link to the survey and a request to complete the survey

The message and informed consent document were in Farsi.

The link took the respondent to a survey engine, keeping the respondent's email address private. As soon as OSU'S Institute Review Board (IRB) released the survey, I distributed the questionnaire via email. I put the survey on surveymonkey.com and opened it survey on January 17, 2008, and closed it one month later on February 17, 2008.

Advantages and Disadvantages of Online Surveys

There are both advantages and disadvantages to online surveys. Dillman (2000) states that online surveys are effective at reducing paper and mailing costs, reducing time required for survey response, and "provide a potential for overcoming international boundaries as significant barriers." Neuman (2006) argues that internet surveys are both fast and inexpensive, as well as visually flexible.

The three major disadvantages are coverage, privacy and verification, and design issues (Neuman, 2006). The first issue is one of access: certain geographical areas and certain demographics of people do not have internet access. I have done my best to reduce the sample to those who will have access to the internet.

The second issue is privacy and verification. Including a link to the survey in an email ensures that the respondent's email will not be recorded. However, I cannot ensure that each respondent only answered the survey once, that every respondent was a woman, or that each respondent was a native of Iran. The entire survey was in Farsi to ensure that only someone literate in Farsi will answer the questions; however, if a respondent is not natively Iranian but is literate in Farsi, s/he had access to the survey as well.

The third issue deals with the design of the survey. Neuman (2006) suggests that screen-by-screen questions and a limited color palette are effective for reading ease. I tried to follow this is my survey design. I also provided clear instructions.

Data Analysis

A survey format allows me to condense the data manageably so that I may run statistical tests on them. I converted data gathered for this study into nominal scales. Questions that dealt with socioeconomic status were grouped together, and questions that deal with style preference were grouped together. These two groups were analyzed using STATA, a statistical program offered by Oregon State University.

In STATA, I used a chi-squared test to analyze the data, in addition to using a simple correlation command to see whether there were any correlations among the variables. Chi-squared tests measure the relationships between variables that are measured on an ordinal or nominal scale, and are preferable to T-tests because this type of test measures means from interval or ratio scales. Chi-squared more effectively analyzed my data because the data is nominal and rank-ordered.

Through simple correlation and analysis using a chi-squared test, I attempted to illustrate whether young urban Iranian women make fashion preferences based on socioeconomic status.

CHAPTER IV

RESULTS

The purpose of this research was to discern the fashion preferences of urban Iranian women. A web survey was used to collect data and the respondent-driven sampling method was used to identify participants.

The survey was broken into three sections: fashion questions, personal demographic information, and family demographic information. There were a total of 29 questions on the survey.

Data was collected using a respondent-driven web-based survey. A total of 23 respondents started the survey, but only 19 respondents completed the entire survey. Though four respondents did not complete the entire survey, the information that they provided was used in data evaluation. With such a small sample size, I could only use simple correlations and chi-squared tests to analyze the data.

Because of the small sample size, it wasn't necessary to use the tenth percentages. Instead of giving specific percentages with the tenth decimal, I rounded up. For percentages below .5, I rounded down; for those above .5, I rounded up.

Survey Results

Each question from the survey is presented with the response percentage for each answer. Questions 10 and 17 were open-ended. When the response was directly related to another question in the survey, the response is given with the appropriate question. Correlations are presented with the research objectives.

Fashion Questions

Questions 1 – 10 deal with the respondents' fashion preferences.

Question 1. Do you purchase your clothing yourself?

The majority of respondents indicated that they do purchase their own clothing. 69 percent (16 out of 23 respondents) reported that they purchase their own clothing; 26 percent (6 out of 23) reported that they purchase the majority of their own clothing, but that their families and/or spouses also give them clothes; only one respondent indicated that her parents purchase her clothing.

Question 2. Where do you get most of your fashion knowledge?

Many of the respondents reported that they learn about fashion mostly from media outlets, with friends as the second source of fashion knowledge (Table 1).

Table 1
Source of fashion knowledge

Source of Fashion Knowledge	Response Percent	Response Count
Friends	35%	8
Media	**39%**	9
Family	13%	3
Other	13%	3
		N=23

Question 3. When you go out with your friends, which of these clothing items do you usually wear over your clothes?

The majority of respondents (83 percent) report that they wear a *roosari* and *manto* (see Figure 3, Appendix D when they go out with their friends (Table 2).

Table 2
Style of hijab worn out with friends

Clothing Item	Response Percent	Response Count
Chador, with roosari/maghnaeh and manto	9%	2
Roosari and manto	**83%**	19
Maghnaeh and manto	4%	1
Other	4%	1
		N=23

Question 4. When you pick out clothing to wear out with your friends, please rank the following in order of importance: cost, trendiness, modesty, and comfort.

Table 3 indicates that, when purchasing or picking out clothing, most respondents indicate that cost, modesty, and comfort are "fairly important" considerations. Most (39 percent) report that trendiness in a garment is "not very important."

Table 3
Rankings of cost, trendiness, modesty, and comfort in potential clothes to wear out with friends

	Very important	Fairly important	Not very important	Not important at all	Rating Average	Response Count Total
Cost	23% (5)	**36% (8)**	27% (6)	14% (3)	2.32	22
Trendiness	22% (5)	30% (7)	**39% (9)**	9% (2)	2.35	23
Modesty	27% (6)	**46% (10)**	23% (5)	5% (1)	2.05	22
Comfort	39% (9)	**52% (12)**	9% (2)	0% (0)	1.70	23

Question 5. When you pick out clothing to wear out with your friends, how important are brand names?

Most respondents (44 percent) indicated that brand names are not important at all when picking out the clothes they wear out with their friends (Table 4).

Table 4
Importance of brand names

	Response Percent	**Response Count**
Very important	13%	3
Fairly important	13%	3
Not very important	30%	7
Not important at all	**44%**	10
		N=23

Question 6. When you pick out an outfit to wear out with your friends, how important is color coordination and matching?

In Table 5, the majority of respondents (70 percent) stated that color coordination and matching clothing is very important to them when they go out with their friends.

Table 5
Importance of color-coordination in outfits

	Response Percent	**Response Count**
Very important	**70%**	16
Fairly important	22%	5
Not very important	9%	2
Not important at all	0%	0
		N=21

Question 7. Which colors do you like to wear out when you go out with your friends?

According to Table 6, 46 percent of respondents say that they wear darker colors sometimes, 64 percent report wearing light colors sometimes, and 65 percent report that they wear bright colors sometimes. From this we can see that there is no overwhelming preference in color, but rather a mixture of different types of colors prevalent in these women's wardrobes.

On question 10 (which was open-ended), which asked respondents about the clothing preferences, many answered that they preferred bright colors: "I prefer clothing with lively colors…;" "Covers you fully, chic, bright colors;" "I like bright and happy clothing…"

Table 6
Color preference in outfits

	Most of the time	Sometimes	Never	Response Count
Darker colors	41% (9)	**46% (10)**	14% (3)	22
Light colors	14% (3)	**64% (14)**	23% (5)	22
Bright colors	26% (6)	**65% (15)**	9% (2)	23

Question 8. Which embellishments do you like on your clothes when you go out with your friends?

The majority of respondents do not like embellishments: 36 percent reported liking "none of the above," while 23 percent reported "I don't like embellishments" (50 percent altogether). In Table 7, it's evident that the embellishments that a few respondents do like are spread out almost completely evenly between lace, prints, appliqués, and embroidery.

Table 7
Embellishment preference

	Response Percent	Response Count
I don't like embellishments.	23%	5
Prints	9%	2
Lace	9%	2
Appliqués	9%	2
Embroidery	14%	3
None of the above	36%	8
		N=22

Question 9. Please choose a word that describes your style best.

Many of the respondents (46 percent) in Table 8 listed themselves as "Classic (I wear clothes without a lot of decoration)." On question 10, which asked respondents to write a few sentences describing their fashion preference, many of them wrote that simple clothes were important: "Simple, clean, and chic;" "I prefer simple and beautiful clothing...;" "In style, without sparkles..."

The second-highest category put themselves as "Casual (I like to be comfortable and ready to go)." Many respondents wrote on question 10 that comfort was very important to them: "Chic and comfortable;" "I prefer my clothing to be up-to-date, brand name, and comfortable;" "Very happy and comfortable clothing."

The third-highest category put themselves as "Modest (I wear clothes that don't draw attention to my femininity)." On question 10, respondents wrote: "Very chic clothing, it should not attract attention...;" "...does not attract attention...;" "Appropriate clothing."

Table 8
Word expressing style preference

Style	Response Percent	Response Count
Casual	23%	5
Modest	14%	3
Classic	**46%**	**10**
Trendy	9%	2
Quality	9%	2
Practical	0%	0
		N=22

Question 10. Please write a few sentences describing what you like to wear when you're out with your friends, and why you like to wear this.

Twenty respondents out of 23 answered this question. I have listed their responses below, in order of respondent:

1. Very chic clothing, it should not attract attention and be comfortable.
2. I like bright and happy clothing, and it is not important that they can be a little unusual and other people avoid wearing them, I would wear them, I do believe somewhat that clothing must cover you fully, since my culture

and customs do not accept every type of dressing. Outside the country, they wear clothing too freely because they believe you cannot wear every clothing in front of Iranian men.

3. Casual: I like to be comfortable and ready to go.
4. Very happy and comfortable clothing.
5. Covers you fully, chic, bright colors.
6. I prefer simple and beautiful clothing. Mainly beauty and uniformity are important.
7. ...
8. I like them to be Comfortable because I want to focus on people who I am with or things that I do rather than "dressing" itself... I like to look good but I don't like to spend a lot of energy on it.
9. Appropriate clothing.
10. In style, without sparkles, does not attract attention. That is by being simple, shows dignity and respectfulness.
11. Chic and comfortable.
12. ??
13. nbl
14. I prefer clothing with lively colors which fit my shape, if it not updated, it is secondary to me, every person has their own type that fits them, I pay attention where I wear certain clothing (even in certain streets and places) I am from a city, hope for your success.
15. Chic, simple, comfortable, covering.

16. Simple, clean, and chic.

17. I don't like to wear hejab, of any kind that we have to in Iran. I don't like to wear sexy stuff either. I like to be seen as a unique lady.

18. I prefer my clothing to be up-to-date, brand name, and comfortable.

19. Simple, and very beautiful and becoming.

20. At first, it must be relax and covered, then I would consider fashion. I can't wear tight jean, I think it would make me sick so even when tight jeans are fashionable, I don't use them, my priority is being relaxed then any thing else.

Questions 1-10 focused on the respondents' fashion preferences. From the results, a large amount of the respondents buy their own clothes, and tend to select clothing that is classic, comfortable and with little or no embellishment. Color coordination of garments is very important and shows that they have a wide variety of colors in their wardrobe.

Personal Demographic Questions

Questions 11 – 21 deal with personal demographic information.

Question 11. What is your age?

Most respondents (43 percent) are between the ages of 27-29, as seen in Table 9.

Table 9
Age of respondent

Age	Response Percent	Response Count
21-23	29%	6
24-26	24%	5
27-29	43%	9
30 or over	5%	1
		N=21

Question 12. What is your marital status?

Many of the respondents (47 percent) reported that they are single. No respondents reported themselves to be separated, divorced, or widowed, though these options were available. Table 10 has thus omitted these designations.

Table 10
Marital status of respondent

Status	Response Percent	Response Total
Single	47%	10
Engaged	10%	2
Married	43%	9
		N=21

Question 13. Do you have children?

The overwhelming majority of respondents (95 percent; 20 out of 21) reported that they do not have children. Only one respondent (5 percent) has children.

Question 14. Do you have health insurance?

The majority of respondents (91 percent: 19 out of 21) do have health insurance (which is considered a indicator of wealth and thus high income status), and the majority of those who had insurance have it through their family (43 percent). Only two respondents out of 21 (10 percent) do not have insurance, according to Table 11.

Table 11
Health insurance of respondent

Health Insurance & Source	Response Percent	Response Total
Yes, via work	29%	6
Yes, via family	**43%**	9
Yes, via spouse	19%	4
No insurance	10%	2
		N=21

Question 15. Do you have internet access at home?

Out of 21 respondents, 19 have access to the internet at home (91 percent); two out of 21 respondents (10 percent) do not.

Question 16. If you do not have internet access at home, where do you access the internet?

Ten out of 23 respondents skipped this question, most likely because they have internet access at home. Of those who answered, 46 percent responded that they access the internet at the university (Table 12).

Table 12
Respondent's internet sources

Internet Source	Response Percent	Response Count
Library	8%	1
University	**46%**	6
Internet Café	15%	2
Other	23%	3
Not applicable	8%	1
		N=13

Question 17. Which city in Iran do you live in?

Twenty respondents completed this question. Out of 20, 11 (55 percent) reported that they currently live in Tehran, the capital city. Two respondents (10 percent) reported living in Mashhad, another large urban center in Iran. Others were scattered around smaller cities in Iran.

Question 18. Who do you live with?

Many of the respondents (40 percent) live with a spouse. No respondents chose the options of living with "extended family members," "spouse and spouse's extended family," or "spouse and members of my [the respondent's] family." Thus, these were left out of the results in Table 13.

Table 13
Respondent's housemate status

Respondent Lives With…	Response Percent	Response Total
Parents	25%	5
Parents & grandparents	5%	1
Roommates	10%	2
Alone	20%	4
Spouse	**40%**	8
		N=20

Question 19. What is the highest level of education you have completed?

A large body of respondents (48 percent) hold master's degrees. Though the question gave respondents options ranging from no formal education to post-doctorate, the above three answers were the only ones chosen (and have thus been omitted from results in Table 14), and only two out of 23 respondents skipped this question. Thus, from this data, we can see that this group of respondents is very highly educated.

Table 14
Respondent's level of education

Education	Response Percent	Response Count
Bachelor's degree	38%	8
Master's degree	**48%**	10
Doctorate	14%	3
		N=21

Question 20. What is your employment status?

According to Table 15, most respondents (48 percent) are employed outside of the home, while the second-largest group of respondents is students.

Table 15
Respondent's employment status

Employment	Response Percent	Response Count
Homemaker	5%	1
Student	43%	9
Self-employed	5%	1
Employed outside the home	48%	10
		N=21

Question 21. What is your monthly personal income after taxes?

Most of the respondents (37 percent) earn an income of between 1,000,001- 5,000,000 rials per month. The second-largest group preferred not to answer (N=6 in Table 16). The majority of respondents fall within the lowest income group (500,000 rials or less to 7,200,000 rials per month).

Table 16
Respondent's monthly income

Income per month	Response Percent	Response Count
500,000 rials or less	21%	4
1,000,001 - 5,000,000 rials	37%	7
5,000,000 - 7,000,000 rials	5%	1
9,000,001 - 12,000,000 rials	5%	1
Prefer not to answer	32%	6
		N=19

Family Demographic Questions

Questions 22 – 29 deal with family demographic information.

Question 22. What is the highest level of education your mother has completed?

Several of the respondents (29 percent) reported that their mothers had earned an associate's degree. The rest of education levels are almost evenly spread out, evident in Table 17.

Table 17
Education level of respondent's mother

Mother's Level of Education	Response Percent	Response Count
No formal education	9%	2
Elementary	14%	3
High school	19%	4
Associate's degree	**29%**	6
Bachelor's degree	19%	4
Doctorate	10%	2
		N=21

Question 23. What is the highest level of education your father has completed?

In Table 18, the majority of respondents reported that their father earned either a high school degree (29 percent) or a bachelor's degree (29 percent).

Table 18
Education level of respondent's father

Father's Level of Education	Response Percent	Response Count
Elementary	9%	1
Middle school	14%	3
High school	**29%**	6
Associate's degree	10%	2
Bachelor's degree	**29%**	6
Master's degree	14%	3
		N=21

Question 24. If you are married, what is the highest level of education your spouse has completed?

Most of the respondents (37 percent) are not married, as seen in Table 19. But of those who are married, their husbands had earned either a bachelor's degree (21 percent) or a master's degree (21 percent).

Table 19
Education level of respondent's spouse

Spouse's Level of Education	Response Percent	Response Count
High school	5%	1
Bachelor's degree	21%	4
Master's degree	21%	4
Doctorate	11%	2
Not married	37%	7
Prefer not to answer	5%	1
		N=19

Question 25. What is your mother's employment status?

In Table 20, the majority of respondents reported that their mothers work inside the home as homemakers (57 percent).

Table 20
Employment status of respondent's mother

Mother's Employment	Response Percent	Response Count
Homemaker	57%	12
Employed outside the home	19%	4
Retired	24%	5
		N=21

Question 26. What is your father's employment status?

As seen in Table 21, one-third of respondents reported that their fathers are self-employed (33 percent) and one-third reported their father is employed outside the home (33 percent).

Table 21
Employment status of respondent's father

Father's Employment	Response Percent	Response Count
Self-employed	**33%**	7
Employed outside the home	**33%**	7
Retired	29%	6
None of the above	5%	1
		N=21

Question 27. What is your spouse's employment status?

Many of respondents are not married, evident in Table 22. Of those that are married, 35 percent reported that their spouse is employed outside the home.

Table 22
Employment status of respondent's spouse

Spouse's Employment	Response Percent	Response Count
Self-employed	5%	1
Employed outside the home	35%	7
Retired	5%	1
None of the above	10%	2
Respondent not married	**45%**	9
		N=20

Question 28. What is your parents' monthly household income after taxes?

In Table 23, most of the respondents (26 percent) preferred not to answer the question. Of those who did, 21 percent reported their parents' monthly income as 1,000,001 – 5,000,000 rials. The majority of respondents parents' fell within the lowest income group, though their wealth was distributed more evenly than the respondents' themselves.

Table 23
Monthly household income of respondent's parents

Parents' income per month	Response Percent	Response Count
500,001 – 1,000,000 rials	5%	1
1,000,001 – 5,000,000 rials	21%	4
5,000,000 -- 7,200,000 rials	16%	3
7,200,001 -- 9,000,000 rials	5%	1
9,000,001 – 12,000,000 rials	5%	1
12,000,001 – 19,500,000 rials	16%	3
19,500,000 rials or more	5%	1
Prefer not to answer	**26%**	5
		N=19

Question 29. If you are married, what is your spouse's monthly income after taxes?

The majority of respondents are not married; of those who were, the 21 percent reported their spouse's monthly income as between 7,200,001 – 9,000,000 rials, as reported in Table 24. The married respondents' wealth was evenly distributed between the lowest income group and the middle income group: five respondents fell within the former, and five respondents fell within the latter.

Table 24
Monthly income of respondent's spouse

Spouse's income per month	Response Percent	Response Count
500,001 – 1,000,000 rials	5%	1
1,000,001 – 5,000,000 rials	16%	3
5,000,000 – 7,200,000 rials	5%	1
7,200,001 – 9,000,000 rials	21%	4
9,000,001 – 12,000,000 rials	5%	1
Not married	47%	9
		N=19

Data Summary

From the data outlined above, I compiled a profile of the average urban Iranian woman that responded to my survey. The average urban Iranian woman respondent is between 27 – 29 years old, lives in Tehran, and has a master's degree. She is not married, has no children, and is employed outside the home, earning a salary which falls within the lowest income bracket (500,000 rials or less to 7,200,000 rials per month, which is approximately $770.22 to $53.49 or less per month). If she is married, she and her spouse have a 50 percent chance of being in either the lowest income bracket or the middle income bracket (7,200,000 – 12,000,000 rials per month, which is approximately $770.22 - $1,283.70 per month). Her parents will most likely have an income that falls within the same lower income bracket.

According to the data, this average respondent wears a *roosari* and *manto* (i.e., a headscarf and overcoat, which she most likely purchased herself) when she goes out with her friends, and gets most of her fashion knowledge from the media. While brand names are not important to her, making sure her outfit is color-coordinated is very important, and she would describe her style as "classic."

Research Objectives and Hypothesis

Objective 1: To determine the socioeconomic status of 15 – 30 year old urban Iranian women.

The data gathered indicates that the respondents were aged 21 – 29. Thus, our data will concentrate on the socioeconomic status of these women, rather than the larger age range of 15 – 30.

Objective 2: To determine what *hijab* styles young urban Iranian women prefer in a public social setting.

The data suggests that women aged 21 – 29, who are highly educated and regular internet users, overwhelmingly prefer the *roosari* and *manto* combination when going out with their friends, and that color coordination is extremely important in fashions these women choose. But this finding should be contextualized within the limited sample size.

Objective 3: To determine if there are correlations between these socioeconomic indicators and *hijab* style preference.

Using the STATA statistics program, correlation and chi-squared tests were used to analyze whether there is a relationship between socioeconomic indicators and *hijab* style preferences.

The correlations among the following variables were compared in Table 25: *hijab* preferences, preferences in cost, trendiness, modesty, comfort, brand names, color coordination and palettes, embellishments, education, income, and parents' income and education, and spouse's income and education.

Table 25
Correlation of outerwear style with fashion preference variable

```
. pwcorr  outerwear cost trendiness modesty comfort brand matching darkcolor
lightcolor brightcolor embellish edu income momedu dadedu sedu pincome sincome, obs
sig star(.05)
```

	outerw~r	cost	trendi~s	modesty	comfort	brand	matching
outerwear	1.0000						
	23						
cost	0.4727*	1.0000					
	0.0263						
	22	22					
trendiness	0.2241	0.0430	1.0000				
	0.3040	0.8494					
	23	22	23				
modesty	0.0000	0.0586	-0.1919	1.0000			
	1.0000	0.7955	0.3922				
	22	22	22	22			
comfort	-0.4705*	-0.2795	-0.1720	0.0000	1.0000		
	0.0235	0.2078	0.4326	1.0000			
	23	22	23	22	23		

	outerw~r	cost	trendi~s	modesty	comfort	brand	matching
brand	0.2244	0.0505	0.7079*	-0.1767	-0.0468	1.0000	
	0.3033	0.8232	0.0002	0.4315	0.8322		
	23	22	23	22	23	23	
matching	0.2632	-0.2501	0.3119	0.2914	-0.1778	0.3557	1.0000
	0.2249	0.2615	0.1473	0.1882	0.4170	0.0958	
	23	22	23	22	23	23	23
darkcolor	0.2677	-0.0198	0.5002*	0.1422	-0.0684	0.1929	-0.0231
	0.2284	0.9322	0.0178	0.5386	0.7625	0.3897	0.9187
	22	21	22	21	22	22	22
lightcolor	0.2589	0.1856	0.4358*	-0.0890	-0.0562	0.4514*	0.3989
	0.2446	0.4206	0.0426	0.7014	0.8038	0.0350	0.0659
	22	21	22	21	22	22	22
brightcolor	-0.3965	-0.3846	-0.3718	-0.2973	0.4699*	-0.1353	-0.2264
	0.0611	0.0772	0.0807	0.1790	0.0237	0.5384	0.2989
	23	22	23	22	23	23	23
embellish	0.3175	0.4506*	0.1387	0.1534	-0.3044	0.3141	0.0035
	0.1500	0.0404	0.5381	0.5068	0.1684	0.1546	0.9876
	22	21	22	21	22	22	22
edu	-0.2133	-0.1069	-0.0476	0.5117*	0.3615	-0.2960	-0.1421
	0.3531	0.6538	0.8376	0.0211	0.1073	0.1926	0.5390
	21	20	21	20	21	21	21
income	-0.1533	-0.4505	0.0594	0.6562*	0.2979	-0.0048	0.5488
	0.6172	0.1224	0.8471	0.0149	0.3229	0.9875	0.0521
	13	13	13	13	13	13	13
momedu	0.2030	0.2754	0.2062	-0.1216	-0.2661	0.5125*	0.2634
	0.3776	0.2398	0.3698	0.6096	0.2437	0.0175	0.2486
	21	20	21	20	21	21	21
dadedu	0.3227	0.3347	0.2246	-0.2371	-0.2266	0.3780	0.1777
	0.1537	0.1492	0.3277	0.3141	0.3233	0.0911	0.4409
	21	20	21	20	21	21	21

(Continued)

```
      sedu |   0.1604   0.5368  -0.0622   0.6013   0.1288   0.2659   0.1336
           |   0.6376   0.0886   0.8557   0.0504   0.7059   0.4293   0.6953
           |       11       11       11       11       11       11       11
           |
   pincome |   0.1761   0.4754  -0.0700   0.2148   0.1547   0.2717   0.3824
           |   0.5470   0.0858   0.8121   0.4607   0.5975   0.3473   0.1772
           |       14       14       14       14       14       14       14
           |
   sincome |   0.3004  -0.0273   0.1547   0.0273   0.0117   0.0087   0.2458
           |   0.3991   0.9403   0.6695   0.9403   0.9744   0.9810   0.4937
           |       10       10       10       10       10       10       10
           |
           | darkco~r lightc~r bright~r embell~h      edu   income   momedu
-----------+------------------------------------------------------------
 darkcolor |   1.0000
           |
           |       22
           |
lightcolor |  -0.0505   1.0000
           |   0.8234
           |       22       22
           |
brightcolor|  -0.4620* -0.3799   1.0000
           |   0.0304   0.0811
           |       22       22       23
           |
  embellish|   0.0942   0.3166  -0.5063*  1.0000
           |   0.6848   0.1621   0.0162
           |       21       21       22       22
           |
       edu |   0.2796  -0.0136  -0.2902   0.0785   1.0000
           |   0.2325   0.9545   0.2020   0.7351
           |       20       20       21       21       21
           |
    income |   0.2842  -0.0402  -0.2694  -0.0265   0.2979   1.0000
           |   0.3467   0.8962   0.3735   0.9314   0.3229
           |       13       13       13       13       13       13
           |
    momedu |  -0.5318*  0.4293   0.0343   0.3037  -0.3650  -0.3299   1.0000
           |   0.0158   0.0589   0.8826   0.1808   0.1037   0.2710
           |       20       20       21       21       21       13
     dadedu|  -0.4463*  0.4942*  0.0734   0.2637  -0.3542  -0.4688   0.8504*
           |   0.0486   0.0268   0.7518   0.2481   0.1152   0.1061   0.0000
           |       20       20       21       21       21       13       21
           |
      sedu |  -0.0485   0.4034  -0.2806   0.0758   0.0872   0.1939   0.4261
           |   0.8875   0.2186   0.4032   0.8246   0.7987   0.6455   0.1913
           |       11       11       11       11       11        8       11
           |
   pincome |  -0.3797   0.5543* -0.0320   0.3306   0.0746  -0.1333   0.4954
           |   0.1806   0.0397   0.9136   0.2483   0.8000   0.6795   0.0717
           |       14       14       14       14       14       12       14
           |
   sincome |   0.3057   0.5496  -0.2890  -0.1053   0.0384  -0.2607   0.1264
           |   0.3903   0.0999   0.4179   0.7721   0.9162   0.5329   0.7279
           |       10       10       10       10       10        8       10
           |
           |   dadedu     sedu  pincome  sincome
-----------+------------------------------------
    dadedu |   1.0000
           |
           |       21
           |
      sedu |   0.2077   1.0000
           |   0.5399
           |       11       11
           |
   pincome |   0.5607*  0.4869   1.0000
           |   0.0370   0.1536
           |       14       10       14
                            (Continued)
```

```
  sincome |   0.0427    0.4763   -0.2899    1.0000
          |   0.9068    0.1640    0.4166
          |       10        10        10        10
```

To decode this huge table, here is a diagram:

```
pwcorr  health edu, obs sig  <-(command for Stata program)
             |    health      edu
-------------+-------------------
      health |   1.0000
             |
             |       21
             |
         edu |   0.1873   <-(relationship)
             |   0.4161   <-(significance level)
             |       21   <-(amount of observations included)
```

The correlations with asterisks next to them have correlative significance using a .05 alpha level. If a correlation does not have a star, then there is no significant relationship between the two variables.

We will only look at asterisked correlations that look at correlations between socioeconomic data and style preference data. The variables relationships we will look at, along with their correlations, are these:

- Type of outerwear (*hijab*) in correlation to importance of cost. There is a positive correlation between the type of *hijab* and the importance of a garment's cost. (r=.47, p<.03)

- Importance of modesty in correlation to income. There is a positive correlation between the importance of modesty and income: the higher one's income, the higher one puts an emphasis on modesty. (r=.66, p<.01)

- Importance of modesty in correlation to education level. There is a positive correlation between education and emphasis on modesty: the more education one has, the more emphasis one puts on modest clothing. (r=.51, p<.02)

- Importance of brand names in correlation to mother's education. There is a positive correlation between these two variables: the more education a mother has, the more her daughter is likely to place importance on brand names. (r=.51, p<.02)
- Preference for dark colors in correlation to mother's education. There is a negative correlation between dark color preference and a mother's education level: the more education a mother has, the less her daughter is likely to prefer dark-colored clothing. (r= -.53, p<.02)
- Preference for dark colors in correlation to father's education. There is a negative correlation between these two: the more education a father has, the less like his daughter is to prefer dark-colored clothing. (r= -.45, p<.05)
- Preference for light colors in correlation to father's education. There is a positive correlation between light color preference and father's education: the more education a father has, the more likely his daughter is to prefer light-colored clothing. (r=.49, p<.03)
- Preference for light colors in correlation to parents' income. There is a positive correlation between these two variables: the higher her parents' income, the more likely a respondent is to prefer light colors. (r=.55, p<.04)

On these variable relationships, we will perform a chi-squared test to determine whether there is a significant relationship between these variables.

In Table 26, we compare the *hijab* preference and importance of cost.

Table 26
Chi-squared of hijab preference and cost importance

```
. tab outerwear cost, chi2 all

                |              cost
      outerwear | very impo fairly im not very unimporta |   Total
----------------+--------------------------------------+---------
        chador+ |     1         1         0         0  |      2
roosari + manto |     4         7         5         2  |     18
magnaeh + manto |     0         0         1         0  |      1
          other |     0         0         0         1  |      1
----------------+--------------------------------------+---------
          Total |     5         8         6         3  |     22

          Pearson chi2(9) =  10.6944   Pr = 0.297
   likelihood-ratio chi2(9) =  8.9217   Pr = 0.445
              Cramér's V =   0.4025
                   gamma =   0.7966   ASE = 0.143
           Kendall's tau-b =   0.4049   ASE = 0.128
```

The chi-square = 10.65. This is not a large number, which could mean there is no substantial effect. With a degrees of freedom (DF) = 9 and an alpha level of .05, the critical value is 16.92, which means that a chi-square with a DF of 9 must be higher than this number. Since our chi-square is only 10.65, this means that there is no significant relationship: the importance of clothing cost does not affect *hijab* style preference.

The second correlation we'll look at it the importance of modest clothing in relation to education levels, shown in Table 27.

Table 27
Chi-squared of modesty and education variables

```
. tab modesty edu, chi2 all

                   |              edu
           modesty | bachelor' master's doctorate |   Total
-------------------+------------------------------+---------
    very important |     4         2         0   |      6
  fairly important |     3         6         1   |     10
not very important |     1         1         1   |      3
       unimportant |     0         0         1   |      1
-------------------+------------------------------+---------
             Total |     8         9         3   |     20

          Pearson chi2(6) =   9.5278   Pr = 0.146
   likelihood-ratio chi2(6) =  8.2278   Pr = 0.222
              Cramér's V =   0.4881
                   gamma =   0.6235   ASE = 0.238
           Kendall's tau-b =   0.4241   ASE = 0.188
```

The chi-square value is 9.53. For a chi-square with a df = 6 and an alpha level of .05, the critical region lies on 12.59. Since 12.59 > 9.53, there is no significant relationship between modesty and education levels, despite a correlation.

Now, we look at the importance of modest clothing as it relates to the respondent's income level (Table 28).

Table 28
Chi-squared of modesty and income variables

```
. tab modesty income, chi2 all

                   |              income
          modesty  | 500,000 r  1,000,001  5,000,000  9,000,001 |   Total
-------------------+--------------------------------------------+--------
   very important |      2           1           0          0   |      3
 fairly important |      2           5           0          0   |      7
not very important|      0           1           1          1   |      3
-------------------+--------------------------------------------+--------
            Total |      4           7           1          1   |     13

          Pearson chi2(6) =   9.7279   Pr = 0.137
   likelihood-ratio chi2(6) =  9.5691   Pr = 0.144
              Cramér's V =    0.6117
                   gamma =    0.8889   ASE = 0.132
            Kendall's tau-b = 0.6275   ASE = 0.162
```

The chi-square here is 9.73. Again, we have a df = 6, which means that the critical value is 12.59, and is higher than our chi-square value. Thus, there is no significant relationship between the respondent's income and the importance of modest clothing.

Looking at the correlation between the respondent's mother's education and preference for brand names in Table 29, we see that the chi-square value is 20.71.

Table 29
Chi-squared of mother's education and brand importance

```
. tab brand momedu, chi2 all

                   |                            momedu
            brand  | no formal elementar high scho associate bachelor'  master's |  Total
-------------------+------------------------------------------------------------+------
    very important |     0         1         1         1         0         0    |    3
   fairly important|     0         1         1         0         0         0    |    2
not very important |     2         0         2         1         1         0    |    6
       unimportant |     0         1         0         1         3         3    |   10
-------------------+------------------------------------------------------------+------
            Total  |     2         3         4         3         4         3    |   21

                   |  momedu
            brand  | doctorate |  Total
-------------------+-----------+--------
    very important |     0     |    3
   fairly important|     0     |    2
not very important |     0     |    6
       unimportant |     2     |   10
-------------------+-----------+--------
            Total  |     2     |   21

        Pearson chi2(18) =  20.7083   Pr = 0.294
 likelihood-ratio chi2(18) =  24.9531   Pr = 0.126
             Cramér's V =   0.5733
                 gamma =   0.6515   ASE = 0.146
          Kendall's tau-b =   0.5205   ASE = 0.112
```

For a chi-square of 20.71, with a df = 18 and an alpha level of .05, our critical region lies just a few points higher, at 28.87. Since 28.87 > 20.71, we can determine that there is no significant relationship between a mother's education and her daughter's preference for brand names.

We also look at the mother's education and its effect on the respondents' preference for dark colors in her clothing. In Table 30, we see that the chi-square value is 17.45.

Table 30
Chi-squared of mother's education and preference for dark colors

```
. tab darkcolor momedu, chi2 all

                |                              momedu
     darkcolor  | no formal  elementar  high scho  associate  bachelor'  master's
     doctorate  |    Total
----------------+--------------------------------------------------------------------
        always  |     0          1          2          0          2          2
     1 |     8
     sometimes  |     0          1          2          2          2          1
     1 |     9
         never  |     2          1          0          0          0          0
     0 |     3
----------------+--------------------------------------------------------------------
         Total  |     2          3          4          2          4          3
     2 |    20

          Pearson chi2(12) =   17.4537   Pr = 0.133
    likelihood-ratio chi2(12) =   16.1428   Pr = 0.185
               Cramér's V =    0.6606
                    gamma =   -0.5229   ASE = 0.228
           Kendall's tau-b =   -0.3953   ASE = 0.187
```

With an alpha level of .05 and a df = 12, we see the critical region lies over 21.03, which is a larger value than our value of 17.45. Thus, there is no significant relationship between a mother's education and her daughter's preference for dark-colored clothing.

Now, we'll look at the father's education and its impact on both dark colors (Table 31) and light colors (Table 32). First, dark colors:

Table 31
Chi-squared of father's education and preference for dark colors

```
. tab darkcolor dadedu, chi2 al

                |                       dadedu
     darkcolor  | elementar  middle sc  high scho  bachelor'  master's  |  Total
----------------+-----------------------------------------------------+--------
        always  |     0          2          0          4          2    |     8
     sometimes  |     0          0          4          3          2    |     9
         never  |     1          1          1          0          0    |     3
----------------+-----------------------------------------------------+--------
         Total  |     1          3          5          7          4    |    20

          Pearson chi2(8) =   13.9603   Pr = 0.083
    likelihood-ratio chi2(8) =   16.4875   Pr = 0.036
               Cramér's V =    0.5908
                    gamma =   -0.4455   ASE = 0.267
           Kendall's tau-b =   -0.3313   ASE = 0.206
```

Our chi-square is 13.96. With a df = 8, and an alpha level of .05, our critical level lies above 15.51, which is just a few points higher than our value of 13.96. We can conclude that there is no significant relationship between a father's education and his daughter's preference for dark clothing.

As for light clothing, we see similar results:

Table 32
Chi-squared of father's education and preference for light clothing

```
. tab lightcolor dadedu, chi2 all

                            dadedu
lightcolor | elementar  middle sc  high scho  bachelor'  master's |    Total
-----------+--------------------------------------------------------+----------
    always |         0         1          1          0         0 |        2
 sometimes |         1         2          4          3         3 |       13
     never |         0         0          0          4         1 |        5
-----------+--------------------------------------------------------+----------
     Total |         1         3          5          7         4 |       20

         Pearson chi2(8) =   9.4286   Pr = 0.307
 likelihood-ratio chi2(8) =  11.3911   Pr = 0.181
              Cramér's V =   0.4855
                   gamma =   0.6000   ASE = 0.164
          Kendall's tau-b =   0.3900   ASE = 0.121
```

With such a low chi-square (9.43), it is inevitable that there is no significant relationship between the father's education and his daughter's preference for light clothing.

Looking at Table 33, we compare whether light colors are dependent on the parent's income:

Table 33
Chi-squared of parent's income and preference for light colors

```
. tab lightcolor pincome, chi2 all

                                        pincome
 lightcolor | 500,001 - 1,000,001 5,000,000 7,200,000 9,000,001 12,000,00 19,500,00 |
 Total
------------+------------------------------------------------------------------+--------
     always |    0         1         0         0         0         0         0 |
 1
  sometimes |    1         3         2         1         1         2         0 |
 10
      never |    0         0         0         1         0         1         1 |
 3
------------+------------------------------------------------------------------+--------
      Total |    1         4         2         2         1         3         1 |
 14

          Pearson chi2(12) =   9.3722   Pr = 0.671
 likelihood-ratio chi2(12) =  10.1599   Pr = 0.602
               Cramér's V =   0.5786
                    gamma =   0.7838   ASE = 0.157
           Kendall's tau-b =   0.4944   ASE = 0.132
```

Our chi-square is 9.37, which is an incredibly small number for df = 12. With an alpha level of .05, the critical value of a chi-square distribution for df = 12 is 21.03, which is much larger than our value of 9.37. Thus there is no significant relationship between preference for light color and parental income.

All results should be received in context of a small sample size.

Post-Hoc Tests

After examining the data and running correlations and chi-squared tests, I ran a post-hoc test as well.

Since the data is almost evenly distributed between single and married respondents, I compared the two groups in their fashion preferences. First, I ran correlation between the variable "marital" and the variables outerwear, cost, modesty, trendiness, comfort, brand, matching, darkcolor, lightcolor, and brightcolor.

Table 34
Correlation between marital and fashion preference variables

```
. pwcorr marital  outerwear cost modesty trendiness comfort brand matching
darkcolor lightcolor brightcolor
> embellish, obs sig star(.05)
```

	marital	outerw~r	cost	modesty	trendi~s	comfort	brand
marital	1.0000						
	21						
outerwear	-0.0717	1.0000					
	0.7575						
	21	23					
cost	0.1300	0.4727*	1.0000				
	0.5849	0.0263					
	20	22	22				
modesty	-0.1936	0.0000	0.0586	1.0000			
	0.4135	1.0000	0.7955				
	20	22	22	22			
trendiness	0.1821	0.2241	0.0430	-0.1919	1.0000		
	0.4296	0.3040	0.8494	0.3922			
	21	23	22	22	23		
comfort	0.0000	-0.4705*	-0.2795	0.0000	-0.1720	1.0000	
	1.0000	0.0235	0.2078	1.0000	0.4326		
	21	23	22	22	23	23	
brand	-0.0775	0.2244	0.0505	-0.1767	0.7079*	-0.0468	1.0000
	0.7386	0.3033	0.8232	0.4315	0.0002	0.8322	
	21	23	22	22	23	23	23
matching	-0.3982	0.2632	-0.2501	0.2914	0.3119	-0.1778	0.3557
	0.0738	0.2249	0.2615	0.1882	0.1473	0.4170	0.0958
	21	23	22	22	23	23	23
darkcolor	0.4678*	0.2677	-0.0198	0.1422	0.5002*	-0.0684	0.1929
	0.0375	0.2284	0.9322	0.5386	0.0178	0.7625	0.3897
	20	22	21	21	22	22	22
lightcolor	-0.0615	0.2589	0.1856	-0.0890	0.4358*	-0.0562	0.4514*
	0.7968	0.2446	0.4206	0.7014	0.0426	0.8038	0.0350
	20	22	21	21	22	22	22
brightcolor	-0.1568	-0.3965	-0.3846	-0.2973	-0.3718	0.4699*	-0.1353
	0.4973	0.0611	0.0772	0.1790	0.0807	0.0237	0.5384
	21	23	22	22	23	23	23
embellish	-0.0813	0.3175	0.4506*	0.1534	0.1387	-0.3044	0.3141
	0.7259	0.1500	0.0404	0.5068	0.5381	0.1684	0.1546
	21	22	21	21	22	22	22

The chart shows that the only correlation is between "marital" and "darkcolor." The correlation is a positive one, meaning that if a respondent is married, she is more likely to prefer dark colors ($r = .47$, $p < .04$).

To see whether there is any significant relationship, I will run a chi-squared test (Table 35).

Table 35
Chi-squared test of marital status and preference for dark colors

```
. tab marital darkcolor, chi2 all

           |          darkcolor
   marital |   always  sometimes      never |     Total
-----------+---------------------------------+----------
    single |        6          5          0 |        11
   married |        2          4          3 |         9
-----------+---------------------------------+----------
     Total |        8          9          3 |        20

         Pearson chi2(2) =   4.9607   Pr = 0.084
  likelihood-ratio chi2(2) = 6.1629   Pr = 0.046
              Cramér's V =   0.4980
                   gamma =   0.7015   ASE = 0.235
         Kendall's tau-b =   0.4259   ASE = 0.175
```

Our chi-square is 4.96, which falls short of the required 5.99 for an alpha level of .05 with a df=2. Thus, there is no significant relationship between marital status and a preference for dark colors.

CHAPTER V

SUMMARY AND CONCLUSIONS

In this chapter I provide a summary of the study and will a brief discussion of the results, conclusions, implications, and recommendations.

Summary

The purpose of this study was to observe the fashion preferences of urban Iranian women and see whether their socio-economic status had any effect on their *hijab* style preferences. A web-based survey was used and distributed by a respondent-generated sampling technique. Twenty-three Iranian women responded to questions on the survey and 19 completed the entire questionnaire.

Since the sample size was so small, the most interesting results were in the resulting percentages and correlations. Despite the prevalent image of Iranian women in engulfing black chadors (large veils that cover the entire body), 82.6% of the respondents preferred the headscarf and overcoat combination to the chador. Brand names are not important to the majority (43.5%) of urban Iranian women, but color-coordination and matching outfits are, according to 69.6% of respondents. The correlations showed positive correlations between income, education level and importance of modesty in clothing preference (with increasing levels of income and education come increasing levels in the importance of modest clothing).

Research Objectives and Hypothesis Conclusions

Objective 1: To determine the socioeconomic status of 15 – 30 year old urban Iranian women.

The data gathered indicates that the respondents were aged 21 – 29. Thus, the data concentrated on the socioeconomic status of these women, rather than the larger age range of 15 – 30.

The socioeconomic status of the sample may be skewed because many of the respondents are currently university students, and the income data wasn't evenly distributed among different income groups.

As indicated earlier, the average salary of an urban Iranian is around two million rials per month, which falls into the lowest income bracket. The majority of respondents also fell into this income bracket, which means that most of them make average salaries, though they have high levels of education. In the U.S., we (often falsely) equate high levels of education with high-paying jobs. But as Shavarini (2006) indicates, in Iran, high levels of education are equated with social status and not job or salary prestige.

Thus, the socioeconomic status of these women reflects a somewhat privileged socioeconomic status in a bad economy: these women are all very well-educated and thus most likely have higher social statuses than those who are not a highly-educated. But their higher social statuses and education levels don't translate to higher salaries: their incomes and the incomes of their parents are in the lowest (or average) economic bracket. Married women fare only slightly better, often because their income and their spouse's are combined.

Objective 2: To determine what *hijab* styles young urban Iranian women prefer in a public social setting.

The data suggests that women aged 21 – 29 that are highly educated and regularly use the internet overwhelmingly prefer the *roosari* and *manto* combination (see Figure 3, Appendix D) when going out with their friends, and that color coordination is extremely important in fashions these women choose.

Objective 3: To determine if there are correlations between these socioeconomic indicators and *hijab* style preference.

Though correlation tests showed that there were some correlations between certain socio-economic indicators and certain clothing preferences, chi-squared tests were ineffective because of the extremely small sample size.

But the correlations may be indicative of trends that I'm unable to account for my literature review. For example, respondent preference for dark colors declined with an increase of parental education. Because of dark colors' (such as navy and black) association with conservative religious attitudes and government sanction of these colors, a decrease in preference that comes with an increase in parental education may signal more liberal attitudes among the educated class. An increase in respondent preference for bright colors (which are not governmentally sanctioned) when a respondent's father had a higher level of education agrees with this speculation.

Thus, though the data doesn't conclusively prove that the styles Iranian women wear illustrate income differentiation, the colors they choose might indicate different social, religious, and educated attitudes.

Limitations

A limitation in my survey was the small sample size. Only 23 people responded to the survey, and out of 23, only 19 completed the survey. In chapter one, I mentioned that recent crackdowns on dress code might make respondents nervous about the intent behind this survey and could inhibit their participation and/or responses. This definitely could have been a factor in the small response pool.

Internet monitoring could also be behind the respondent's conservative responses. In personal observation, many upper-class, educated young Iranian women in Tehran and other major Iranian cities dress to push the state's boundaries: they wear loose scarves that frequently slip off their head and expose their hair, they wear lots of makeup, they wear very tight clothing, and they attempt to show as much skin as possible. But, looking at the survey responses, this same demographic claims that "comfort" and "does not attract attention" are important personal requirements, rather than "sexiness" or "tight fit" observed in personal experience. Since the IRI monitors internet usage, respondents might have tailored their responses to appear more concerned with fulfilling the legal dress code. They might believe that truthful responses could bring unwanted attention from government officers.

Some of the correlations hinted at a difference between the respondents' answers and their practices. The importance of modesty had positive correlations to both income and education levels, meaning that the more income or education a respondent has, the more important modesty is to her. Again, if the purpose of her clothing is to show off her socioeconomic status with frivolous clothes that toe the line of government modesty requirements, it seems as though the government's idea of modesty and her idea of modesty would be different.

Another limitation to my survey is that all the respondents were highly educated. While there is a high rate of university attendance in most urban areas, there are of course those who do not attend college in any city, and my sample did not capture any of this demographic.

Recommendations

There is very little data on Iranian women's fashion preferences, and so more exploration is needed. It would be more helpful to simply focus on this demographic (urban Iranian women) for exploratory studies in fashion preferences, instead of trying to explore fashion preferences as well as investigate correlations between socio-economic status and style preference.

Adding questions about fashion influences, shopping habits, and even more questions about preferences would improve the study's face validity on style preferences. For example, many women stated that they liked their clothes to be "chic," but did not elaborate. A few questions on what these women consider "chic" would be helpful in the next phase of this study.

Recommendations for Further Study

Since there is almost no data about these women or their fashion preferences in western academia, this is an area rich for further study. Aside from gathering more in-depth data about urban Iranian women's fashion preferences, data about rural Iranian women's fashion is also almost nonexistent, and thus can prove to be a useful study. Cross-cultural comparisons are also a possibility: future studies can compare the fashion preferences of women who live in Iran and Iranian women who live in the U.S. or other countries in the West. Another possibility would be to compare fashion preferences of Iranian women with those of Egyptian women or other women in Middle Eastern countries. Since both Saudi Arabia and Iran have mandatory dress codes, it would be very interesting to compare their *hijab* style preferences.

Another interesting comparison could be made between those who *want* to wear more conservative styles in line with religious beliefs, and those who wear *hijab* because it's mandated by Iranian law.

Implications of This Study

Though it has a small sample size, this study indicates that young, urban Iranian women that have high levels of education, regularly use the internet, and make an average income do not usually wear the *chador* (the black cover which envelops the body). This can help refute the idea that all Iranian women wear the *chador*. The *chador* is often used to symbolize an Iranian woman in the western media; this study can begin to counter this image. This study might also dispel the myth that Iranian women are somehow "outside" of fashion because of the IRI's mandatory dress code.

BIBLIOGRAPHY

Ahmed, L. (1992). *Women and Gender in Islam.* New Haven, CT: Yale University Press.

Ali, S. (2005). Why Here, Why Now? Young Muslim Women Wearing *Hijāb*. *Muslim World, 95*(4). 515-530.

Balasescu, A. (2007). *Haute Couture* in Tehran: Two Faces of an Emerging Fashion Scene. *Fashion Theory, 11*(2/3). 299-318.

Berkey, J. P. (2003). *The Formation of Islam: Religion and Society in the Near East, 600-1800.* New York: Cambridge University Press.

Betteridge, A. H. (1983). To Veil or Not To Veil: A Matter of Protest or Policy. In Nashat, G. (Ed.) *Women and Revolution in Iran* (pp 109-128). Boulder, Colorado: Westview Replica Edition.

Chico, B. (2000). Gender Headwear Traditions in Judaism and Islam. *Dress, 27.* 18-36.

Choksy, J. K. (2003). Women during the Transition from Sasanian to Early Islamic Times. In Nashat, G. & Beck, L. (Eds.) *Women in Iran from the Rise of Islam to 1800* (pp 48-67). Chicago: University of Illinois Press.

Cole, D. & Ahmadi, S. (2003). Perspectives and Experiences of Muslim Women Who Veil on College Campuses. *Journal of College Student Development, 44*(1). 47- 66.

Dillman, D. A. (2000). *Mail and Internet surveys: The tailored design method,* 2nd ed. New York: Wiley.

Eid, P. (2002). Post-Colonial Identity and Gender in the Arab World: The Case of the Hijab. *Atlantis, 26*(2). 39-51.

El Guindi, F. (1999).*Veil: Modesty, Privacy and Resistance.* Oxford: Berg.

El Guindi, F. (2005). Gendered Resistance, Feminist Veiling, Islamic Feminism. *Ahfad Journal, 22*(1). 53-78.

Forbes Manz, B. (2003). Women in Timurid Dynastic Politics. In Nashat, G. and Beck, L. (Eds.) *Women in Iran from the Rise of Islam to 1800* (pp 121-139). Chicago: University of Illinois Press.

Fung, M. S. C., and Yuen, M. (2002). Clothing interest among Chinese adolescent girls in Hong Kong in relation to socioeconomic status. *Psychological Reports, 90*(2). 387-390.

Haddad, Y. Y. (1984). Islam, Women and Revolution in Twentieth-Century Arab Thought. *The Muslim World*, LXXIV(3/4). 137-160.

Hessini, L. (1994). Wearing the Hijab in Contemporary Morocco: Choice and Identity. In Göçek, F. M. & Balaghi, S. (Eds). *Reconstructing Gender in the Middle East: Tradition, Identity, and Power* (pp 40-56). New York: Columbus University Press.

Hillenbrand, C. (2003). Women in the Seljuq Period. In Nashat, G. and Beck, L. (Eds.) *Women in Iran from the Rise of Islam to 1800* (pp 103-120). Chicago: University of Illinois Press.

Hoodfar, H. (1997) The Veil in Their Minds and on Our Heads: Veiling Practices and Muslim Women. In Lowe, L. & Lloyd, D. (Eds.) *The Politics of Culture in the Shadow of Capital* (pp 248-279). London: Duke University Press.

Kamiar, M. (2007a). Country Name Calling: The Case of Iran vs. Persia. *FOCUS on Geography, 49*(4). 2-11.

Kamiar, M. (2007b). Timeline of Important Events in Iran, 8,000 BCE to the Present. *FOCUS on Geography, 49*(4). 1.

Keddie, N. R. (1980). *Iran: Religion, Politics, and Society*. Totowa, New Jersey: Frank Cass and Co. Ltd.

Keddie, N. (2000). Women in Iran since 1979. *Social Research, 67*(2). 405-438.

Khalifa, R. (2007) Sura - 24 Light (Al-Nur). Retrieved August 10, 2007, from The Authorized English Translation of the Qur'an Website: http://www.submission.org/suras/sura24.html.

Lewis, M.A., Dyer, C. L., & Moran, J. D. III. (1985). Parental and peer influences on the clothing purchases of female adolescent consumers as a function of discretionary income. *Journal of Family and Consumer Sciences, 87*. 15-20.

Lurie, A. (1981). *The Language of Clothes*. New York: Random House.

Mahdavi, S. (2004). Women in the Nineteenth Century. In Nashat, G. and Beck, L. (Eds). *Women in Iran from 1800 to the Islamic Republic* (pp 63-84). Chicago: University of Illinois Press.

Mehryar, A. H. & Tashakkori, G. A. (1978). Sex and Parental Education as

Determinants of Marital Aspirations and Attitudes of a Group of Iranian Youth. *Journal of Marriage and the Family, 40*(3). 629-637.

Mehryar, A. H. & Tashakkori, G. A. (1984). A father's education as a determinant of the socio-economic and cultural characteristics of families in a sample of Iranian adolescents. *Sociological Inquiry, 54.* 62-71.

Mojtahed-Zadeh, P. (2007). Iran: An Old Civilization and a New State. *FOCUS on Geography, 49*(4). 20-32.

Momen, M. (1985). *An Introduction to Shi'i Islam: The History and Doctrines of Twelver Shi'ism.* New Haven, CT; Yale University Press.

Moors, A. (2007). Fashionable Muslims: Notions of Self, Religion, and Society in San'a. *Fashion Theory, 11*(2/3). 319-346.

Morgan, D. (1988). *Medieval Persia: 1040-1797.* London & New York: Longman Group UK Limited.

Nashat, G. (2003). Women in Pre-Islamic and Early Islamic Iran. In Nashat, G. and Beck, L. (Eds.) *Women in Iran from the Rise of Islam to 1800* (pp 11-47). Chicago: University of Illinois Press.

Nashat, G. (2004a). Introduction. In Nashat, G. and Beck, L. (Eds). *Women in Iran from 1800 to the Islamic Republic* (pp 1-36). Chicago: University of Illinois Press.

Nashat, G. (2004b). Marriage in the Qajar Period. In Nashat, G. and Beck, L. (Eds). *Women in Iran from 1800 to the Islamic Republic* (pp 37-62). Chicago: University of Illinois Press.

Neuman, W. L. (2006). *Social Research Methods: Qualitative and Quantitative Approaches,* 6th ed. University of Wisconsin at Whitewater: Pearson Education, Inc.

Osella, C., & Osella, F. (2007). Muslim Style in South India. *Fashion Theory, 11*(2/3). 233-252.

Ryan, M. S. (1966). *Clothing: A Study in Human Behavior.* New York: Holt, Rinehart and Winston, Inc.

Seikaly, M. (1998). Women and Religion in Bahrain: An Emerging Identity. In Haddad, Y. Y. & Esposito, J. L. (Eds.) *Islam, Gender, & Social Change* (pp 169-189). Oxford: Oxford University Press.

Shaditalab, J. (2005). Iranian Women: Rising Expectations. *Critique: Critical Middle Eastern Studies, 14*(1). 35-55.

Shavarini, M. K. (2005). The Feminisation of Iranian Higher Education. *Review of Education, 51*. 329-347.

Shavarini, M. K. (2006). Wearing the Veil to College: The Paradox of Higher Education in the Lives of Iranian Women. *International Journal of Middle East Studies, 38*(2). 189-211.

Simmel, G. (1971). "Fashion." In Levine, D. N. (ed.) *On Individuality and Social Forms. Selected Writings* (pp. 294-324). Chicago, IL: University of Chicago Press.

Statistical Centre of Iran. (2000a). Selected Household Socio-Economic Indicators of Iran. *Iran Popin Pages.* Retrieved on October 15, 2007 from: http://www.unescap.org/esid/psis/population/popin/profiles/iran/pub.htm.

Statistical Centre of Iran. (2000b). Status of Youth Nationwide (Socio-economic Characteristics). *Iran Popin Pages.* Retrieved on October 15, 2007 from: http://www.unescap.org/esid/psis/population/popin/profiles/iran/pub.htm.

Statistical Centre of Iran. (2001). Population Data Sheet for Islamic Republic of Iran. *Iran Popin Pages.* Retrieved October 15, 2007 from: http://www.unescap.org/esid/psis/population/popin/profiles/iran/Download%5C2.Jpg

Szuppe, M. (2003). Women in Sixteenth-Century Safavid Iran. In Nashat, G. and Beck, L. (Eds.) *Women in Iran from the Rise of Islam to 1800* (pp 140-169). Chicago: University of Illinois Press.

Veblen, T. (1912). *The Theory of the Leisure Class.* New York: Macmillan.

Welch, S. (1975). Sampling by Referral in a Dispersed Population. *Public Opinion Quarterly, 39*(2). 237-246.

Yahoo! Finance. (n.d.) U.S. Dollar to Iran Rial Exchange Rate. http://finance.yahoo.com/currency/convert?amt=1&from=USD&to=IRR&submit=Convert. Retrieved on October 15, 2007.

Yarshater, E. (1989). When 'Persia' Became 'Iran'. *Iranian Studies: Bulletin of the Society for Iranian Cultural and Social Studies, 22*(1). 62-65.

Yusuf Ali, A. (2001). *The Holy Qur'an.* Lincolnwood, IL: NTC/Contemporary Publishing Company; New Ed edition

APPENDICES

APPENDIX A

INFORMED CONSENT (ENGLISH)

[When the participant clicks on the link to the survey in the email, this is the first page that will show up. This is the informed consent document. The participant will have to click a button signifying her agreement that she has read and understood the informed consent document. Once she clicks the button that signifies her agreement, she will start the web survey.]

You are being invited to take part in a research study conducted by an Oregon State University student. This study is designed to analyze clothing style preferences for social settings in urban Iranian women. The results will explore the effects of socioeconomic status on style preferences. We are studying this because there is a deficiency of research on style preferences of Iranian women in Western academia, and this study will help me complete my Masters thesis.

You are being invited to participate in this study because you are an urban Iranian woman. We are interested in the types of clothes you choose for yourself when you are in public social settings, and why you choose them.

Your participation is voluntary. The survey is estimated to take less than fifteen minutes, and you can exit the survey at any time.

The researchers see no possible risks or benefits to you if you participate in this study. However, we are taking precautions to guarantee your security: the survey is located through a **secure** university server. The information you provide during this research study will be kept confidential to the extent permitted by law. To help protect your confidentiality, **we will not ask for your email or home address, phone numbers, or name.**

If you have any questions about this research project, please contact the researcher, Fatemeh Fakhraie, at her email address: fakhrail@onid.orst.edu.

If you have questions about your rights as a participant, please contact the Oregon State University Institutional Review Board (IRB) Human Protections Administrator at 541-737-4933 or at IRB@oregonstate.edu.

Clicking on the button below and your participation in the survey indicates that you have read through this message and understood it, that your questions have been answered, and that you agree to take part in the study.

[Here there will be a button that says, "I agree and wish to participate." This will take them to the survey's first page.]

INFORMED CONSENT (FARSI)

از شما دعوت میشود که در این پروژه تحقیقاتی و اجتماعی شرکت کنید. این پروژه توسط یک دانشجو ودانشگاه ایالتی اورگان امریکاه انجام میشود.

این تحقیقات در مورد تقاضا و تصمیمات و دلایل مختلف انتخاب لباس خانمهای شهرستانی ایران است.

وبه دو علت انجام میگیرد:

اول-کم بود ویا نبودن اطلاعات اساسی و اجتماعی در مورد انواع انتخابی لباس خانمهای ایرانی.

دو-این پروژه یکی از واحدهای لازم فوق لیسان دانشجو است.

چون شما خانم هستید ودر شهرستان هستید و شما تصمیمات میگیرید درمورا نواع لباسهائی که در مهمانی و در اوقات اجتماعی در بیرون از خانه میپوشید که در این تحقیقات مهم است.

مدت وقت برای اتمام این سئولات حدودن 15 دقیقه میباشد. ودر هر موقه میتوانید که ادامه ندهید. هیچ نوع منفعت یا ضرر برای شما ندارد.

چندین اقداماتی شده که اطلاعاتی که میدهیدناشناس بماند.

هیچگونه اطلاعات شخصی مثل اسم وادرس وادرس کمپیوتر و تلفن در این سئولات نیست.

برای سئولات و اطلات بیشتر در مورد این تحقیقات با خانم فاطمه فخرائی تماس بگیرید.

fakhrail@onid.orst.edu.

برای سئولات مربوط به دانشگاه با دانشگاه ایالتی اورگان تماس بگیرید.

Oregon State University
Institutional Review Board (IRB)
Human Protections Administrator
at 541-737-4933
at IRB@oregonstate.edu.

با انتخاب دکمه قابول میکنید که تمام اطلاعت لازمه خواندید و میفهمید و در این پروجه شرکت میکنید.

APPENDIX B

SURVEY (ENGLISH)

Fashion questions
1. Do you purchase your clothing yourself? [answers in a drop-down box]
No, my parents buy most of my clothing
No, my spouse buys most of my clothing
No, my parents and my spouse buy most of my clothing
No, other people buy my clothing.
Yes, I buy my most of own clothing
Yes, I buy my own clothing, but my parents or spouse buy things for me as well

2. Where do you get most of your fashion knowledge? [dropdown box]
Friends
Media (magazines, television, the internet)
Family
Other

3. When you go **out with your friends**, which of these clothing items do you usually wear over your clothes? [check all that apply]
Chador
Chador with roosari/maghnaeh and manto
Roosari and manto
Magnaeh and manto
Other

4. When you pick out clothing to wear **out with your friends**, please rank the following in order of importance: (1 = Most important, 4 = least important) [each answer will have a drop-down box including the numbers 1-4, which will change according to the respondents' answers]
Cost
Trendiness
Modesty
Comfort

5. When you pick out clothing to **wear out with your friends**, how important are brand names? [drop down box]
Very important
Important
Somewhat important
Not very important
Not important at all

6. When you pick out an outfit to **wear out with your friends,** how important is color coordination and matching? [dropdown box]

Very important
Important
Somewhat important
Not very important
Not important at all

7. What colors do you like to wear out when you go out with your friends? [exclusive circle boxes]
   Darker colors (like dark blue, brown, black)
      Most of the time   Some of the time   Never
   Lighter colors (like grey, white, pastels)
      Most of the time   Some of the time   Never
   Bright colors (like red, yellow, pink, bright blue or green or purple)
      Most of the time   Some of the time   Never

8. Which embellishments do you like on your clothes when you go out with your friends? (check all that apply) [check boxes]
I don't like embellishments
Prints
Lace
Appliqués
Rhinestones
Embroidery
None of the above

9. Please choose a word that describes your style best. [dropdown box]
Casual (I like to be comfortable and ready to go)
Modest (I wear clothes that don't draw attention to my femininity)
Classic (I wear clothes without a lot of decoration)
Trendy (I'm fashionable, with or without designer labels)
Quality (I like to wear the most quality fabrics)
Practical (I dress to be clothed)

10. Please write a few sentences describing what you like to wear **when you're out with your friends**, and why you like to wear this. [short answer space]

Demographic questions
11. What is your age? [these will appear in a drop-down box]
15 or younger
15-17
18-20
21-23
24-26
27-29
30 and above
No answer

12. Marital status: [drop-down box]
Single
Engaged
Married
Separated
Divorced
Widowed
No answer

13. Do you have children? [answers in a drop-down box]
Yes
No
No answer

14. Do you have health insurance? [dropdown box]
Yes, I have a health insurance plan through my place of work.
Yes, I have health insurance under my family's insurance.
Yes, I have health insurance under my spouse's insurance.
No, I do not have health insurance.
No answer

15. Do you have internet access at home? [answers in a drop-down box]
Yes
No
No answer

16. If you do not have internet access at home, where do you access the internet? (check all boxes that apply)
My place of employment
Library
Friend's house
University
Internet Café
Other
No answer

17. Which city in Iran do you live in? [answers will have short space]

18. Who do you live with? [answers in a drop-down box
I live with my parents
I live with my parents and grandparents
I live with extended family members
I live with roommates
I live by myself
I live with my spouse

I live with my spouse and members of my family
I live with my spouse and members of his family
No answer

19. What is the highest level of education you have completed? [drop down box]
No formal education
Elementary school
Middle School
High school
Associate's Degree
Bachelor degree
Master's degree
Doctorate
Post-doctorate
No answer

20. What is your employment status? [dropdown box]
Homemaker
Student
Self-employed
Employed outside the home
No answer

21. What is your monthly personal income after taxes? [dropdown box]
500,000 rials or less
500,001 – 1,000,000 rials
1,000,001 – 5,000,000 rials
5,000,000 -- 7,200,000 rials
7,200,001 -- 9,000,000 rials
9,000,001 – 12,000,000 rials
12,000,001 – 19,500,000 rials
19,500,000 rials or more
Not applicable/I don't want to answer

Family questions

22. What is the highest level of education your mother has completed? [dropdown box]
No formal education
Elementary school
Middle school
High school
Associate's degree
Bachelor's degree
Master's degree
Doctorate
Post-doctorate

No answer

23. What is the highest level of education your father has completed? [dropdown box]
No formal education
Elementary school
Middle school
High school
Associate's degree
Bachelor's degree
Master's degree
Doctorate
Post-doctorate
No answer

24. If you are married, what is the highest level of education your spouse has completed? [drop down box]
No formal education
Elementary school
Middle school
High school
Associate's degree
Bachelor's degree
Master's degree
Doctorate
Post-doctorate
Not applicable/I am not married
No answer

25. What is your mother's employment status? [dropdown box]
Homemaker
Self-employed
She works outside the home.
She is retired
None of the above
No answer

26. What is your father's employment status? [dropdown box]
Self-employed
He works outside the home
He is retired
None of the above
No answer

27. What is your spouse's employment status? [dropdown box]
He is self-employed
He works outside the home

He is retired
None of the above
Not applicable/I am not married
No answer

28. What is your parents' monthly household income after taxes? [dropdown box]
500,001 – 1,000,000 rials
1,000,001 – 5,000,000 rials
5,000,000 -- 7,200,000 rials
7,200,001 -- 9,000,000 rials
9,000,001 – 12,000,000 rials
12,000,001 – 19,500,000 rials
19,500,000 rials or more
I don't want to answer

29. If you are married, what is your spouse's monthly income after taxes? [dropdown box]
500,001 – 1,000,000 rials
1,000,001 – 5,000,000 rials
5,000,000 -- 7,200,000 rials
7,200,001 -- 9,000,000 rials
9,000,001 – 12,000,000 rials
12,000,001 – 19,500,000 rials
19,500,000 rials or more
Not applicable/I am not married
I don't want to answer

Thank you for taking the time to complete this survey. Your responses are helpful and are greatly appreciated.

SURVEY (FARSI)

سؤال های مربوط به لباس

1 –
آیا شما لباس هایتان را خودتان انتخاب می کنید؟
خیر، خانواده ام بیشتر لباس هایم را می خرد
خیر، همسرم بیشتر لباس هایم را می خرد
خیر، خانواده و همسرم بیشتر لباس های من را می خرند
خیر، بقیه برای من لباس می گیرند
بله، من بیشتر لباس هایم را خودم می خرم
بله، من لباس هایم را خودم می خرم ولی والدین یا همسرم هم برای من لباس می گیرند

2-

شما بیشتر اطلاعاتتان را راجع به مد از کجا می آورید؟
دوستان
رسانه (تلویزیون، مجله، اینترنت، غیره)
خانواده
غیره

3-
وقتی که شما با دوستانتان بیرون می روید، کدام یک از این لباس ها را اکثر مواقع روی لباس خود می پوشید؟

چادر
چادر به همراه روسری یا مقنعه و مانتو
روسری و مانتو
مقنعه و مانتو
غیره

4-
وقتی که شما برای بیرون رفتن با دوستانتان لباس تهیه می کنید، کدام یک از موارد زیر برای شما مهم تر است؟ لطفاً از 1 تا 4 این موارد را شماره گذاری کنید به طوری که 1 مهم ترین عنوان و 4 کم اهمیت ترین عنوان باشد.

قیمت لباس
مد بودن لباس
پوشیده بودن لباس
راحتی لباس

5-
وقتی شما برای بیرون رفتن با دوستانتان لباس تهیه می کنید، مارک دار بودن لباس تا چه حد اهمیت دارد؟

خیلی مهم   نسبتاً مهم   کمی مهم   اصلاً مهم نیست

6-
وقتی شما برای ببرون رفتن با دوستانتان لباس انتخاب می کنید، اینکه اجزای لباس شما از نظر رنگ و مدل به هم بیایند چه قدر برای شما اهمیت دارد؟

خیلی مهم   نسبتاً مهم   کمی مهم   اصلاً مهم نیست

7-
وقتی شما با دوستانتان بیرون می روید، چه رنگ هایی ترجیح می دهید به تن کنید؟

رنگ های تیره تر (مانند سورمه ای، قهوه ای، سیاه)
بیشتر اوقات   بعضی اوقات   هیچ وقت

رنگ های کم رنگ (مانند سفید، خاکستری)
بیشتر اوقات   بعضی اوقات   هیچ وقت

رنگ های زنده و روشن (مانند قرمز، زرد، صورتی، آبی روشن، سبز یا بنفش)

بیشتر اوقات   بعضی اوقات   هیچ وقت

8-
وقتی با دوستانتان بیرون می روید، ترجیح می دهید لباس هایتان کدام یک از تزئینات زیر را داشته باشند؟

من اصلاً تزئینات دوست ندارم
طرح چاپی روی لباس
تور
تکه دوزی
نگین
گل دوزی
هیچ کدام از موارد بالا

9-
لطفاً آن کلمه ای که سلیقه شما را بهتر از همه توصیف می کند، انتخاب کنید.

راحت (من دوست دارم که لباس هایم ساده و راحت باشند و همیشه به سرعت برای بیرون رفتن آماده بشوم)
پوشیده (من لباس هایی را ترجیح می دهم که بدن من در آنها نمودی نداشته باشد)
کلاسیک (من لباس هایی می پوشم که خیلی زرق و برق نداشته باشند)
مطابق با مد (من مطابق با مد روز لباس هایم را انتخاب می کنم. چه اینکه لباس هایم مارک های معروف داشته باشند و چه نداشته باشند)
جنس (من لباس هایی دوست دارم که از جنس های فوق العاده خوبی تولید شده باشند)
کاربردی (من تنها می خواهم کارم راه بیفتد و به نکات دیگر در مورد لباسم توجه ندارم)

10-
لطفاً چند جمله راجع به لباس هایی که دوست دارید در هنگام بیرون رفتن با دوستانتان بپوشید بنویسید و دلایلتان را برای این انتخاب ها توضیح دهید.

سؤالات آماری

11-
سن شما چیست؟
15 سال یا کمتر
15 تا 17
18 تا 20
21 تا 23
24 تا 26
27 تا 29
30 به بالا
ترجیح می دهم به این سؤال جواب ندهم

12-
وضعیت تأهل شما؟
مجرد
نامزد
مزدوج

مطلقه
بیوه
ترجیح می دهم به این سؤال جواب ندهم

13-
آیا شما فرزند دارید؟
بله
خیر
ترجیح می دهم به این سؤال جواب ندهم

14-
آیا شما بیمه درمانی دارید؟
بله، من از طریق محل کار به بیمه درمانی دسترسی دارم
بله، من از طریق خانواده ام بیمه درمانی دارم
بله، من از طریق همسرم بیمه درمانی دارم
نه، من بیمه درمانی ندارم
ترجیح می دهم به این سؤال جواب ندهم

15-
آیا شما در خانه به اینترنت دسترسی دارید؟
بله
خیر
ترجیح می دهم به این سؤال جواب ندهم

16-
اگر شما در خانه به اینترنت دسترسی ندارید، در کجا به اینترنت دسترسی پیدا می کنید؟
کتابخانه
خانه دوست
دانشگاه
اینترنت کافه
غیره
ترجیح می دهم به این سؤال جواب ندهم

17-
شهر محل سکونت شما:

18-
با چه کسانی زندگی می کنید؟
با والدین
با والدین و پدربزرگ و مادربزرگ
با وابستگان
با هم اطاقی ها
تنها
با همسر
با همسر و اعضای خانواده خودم
با همسر و اعضای خانواده او
ترجیح می دهم به این سؤال جواب ندهم

19-
بالاترین درجه تحصیلی شما:
تحصیل ندارم
ابتدایی
راهنمایی
دبیرستان
فوق دیپلم
لیسانس
فوق لیسانس
دکتری
فوق دکتری
ترجیح می دهم به این سؤال جواب ندهم

20-
شما به چه نوع کاری اشتغال دارید؟
خانه دار
دانشجو
خویش کارفرما
اشتغال بیرون از خانه
ترجیح می دهم به این سؤال جواب ندهم

21-
حقوق ماهانه شما چه میزان می باشد؟

500,000 ریال یا کمتر
500,001 – 1,000,000 ریال
1,000,001 – 5,000,000 ریال
5,000,000 -- 7,200,000 ریال
7,200,001 -- 9,000,000 ریال
9,000,001 – 12,000,000 ریال
12,000,001 – 19,500,000 ریال
19,500,000 ریال یا بیشتر
ترجیح می دهم به این سؤال جواب ندهم

سؤالات خانواده ای

22-
بالاترین درجه تحصیلی مادر شما چه می باشد؟

تحصیل ندارد
ابتدایی
راهنمایی
دبیرستان
فوق دیپلم
لیسانس

فوق لیسانس
دکتری
فوق دکتری
ترجیح می دهم با این سؤال جواب ندهم

23-
بالاترین درجه تحصیلی پدر شما چه می باشد؟

تحصیل ندارد
ابتدایی
راهنمایی
دبیرستان
فوق دیپلم
لیسانس
فوق لیسانس
دکتری
فوق دکتری
ترجیح می دهم با این سؤال جواب ندهم

24-
اگر شما ازدواج کرده اید، بالاترین درجه تحصیلی همسر شما چه می باشد؟

تحصیل ندارد
ابتدایی
راهنمایی
دبیرستان
فوق دیپلم
لیسانس
فوق لیسانس
دکتری
فوق دکتری
ازدواج نکرده ام
ترجیح می دهم با این سؤال جواب ندهم

25-
مادر شما به چه شغلی اشتغال دارد؟

خانه دار
خویش کارفرما
اشتغال بیرون از خانه
بازنشسته
هیچ کدام از موارد بالا
ترجیح می دهم با این سؤال جواب ندهم

26-
پدر شما به چه شغلی اشتغال دارد؟

خویش کارفرما
اشتغال بیرون از خانه
بازنشسته
هیچ کدام از موارد بالا
ترجیح می دهم با این سؤال جواب ندهم

27-
همسر شما به چه شغلی اشتغال دارد؟

خویش کارفرما
اشتغال بیرون از خانه
بازنشسته
هیچ کدام از موارد بالا
من ازدواج نکرده ام
ترجیح می دهم به این سؤال جواب ندهم

28-
حقوق ماهانه والدین شما چه میزان می باشد؟

500,000 ریال یا کمتر
500,001 – 1,000,000 ریال
1,000,001 – 5,000,000 ریال
5,000,000 -- 7,200,000 ریال
7,200,001 -- 9,000,000 ریال
9,000,001 – 12,000,000 ریال
12,000,001 – 19,500,000 ریال
19,500,000 ریال یا بیشتر
ترجیح می دهم جواب این سؤال را ندهم

29-
اگر ازدواج کرده اید، حقوق ماهانه همسر شما چه میزان می باشد؟

500,000 ریال یا کمتر
500,001 – 1,000,000 ریال
1,000,001 – 5,000,000 ریال
5,000,000 -- 7,200,000 ریال
7,200,001 -- 9,000,000 ریال
9,000,001 – 12,000,000 ریال
12,000,001 – 19,500,000 ریال
19,500,000 ریال یا بیشتر
ترجیح می دهم جواب این سؤال را ندهم
ازدواج نکرده ام

از اینکه وقت گذاشتید و این فرم را پر کردید متشکریم.

APPENDIX C

EMAIL MESSAGE

This is the message I will include with each survey. The Farsi translation is below, followed by the English translation.

اسم من فاطمه فخرائی است. من دانشجویه فوقلیسانس در رشته طرح لباس هستم. و در دانشگاهه ایالتی اورگان در اورگان امریکا میباشم.
این تحقیق درمورد خانمهای جوان ایرانی است و چه طرح لباسهائی مورد انتخبشان است.
من از شما دعوت میکنم که در این تحقیق انتخابی وخصوصی شرکت کنید. واین دعوت وفرم تحقیق را برای 10 تا ازخانمهای دوستیتان بفرستید که تعدادشرکت کننده در تحقیقات زیادتر باشد. این پرسشنامه خصوصیست و هیچ گونه اطلاعاتی وادرس کمپیوتری بیرون داده نمیشود. لطفان هرچه زودتر این پرسش نامه را تمام کنید.

با انتخاب دکمه دراین پروجه شرکت میکنیدو صفحه پرسشنام میروید..

قبلان از همکار شما تشکر میکنم.

فاطمه فخرائی

"Hello. My name is Fatemeh Fakhraie and I am a graduate student in Apparel Design at Oregon State University in Oregon, U.S.A. I am conducting research among young Iranian women to ascertain their style preferences. I ask for your participation in the survey, and I ask that you forward this email to 10 of your female friends so that I may receive more responses.

Your personal information and email address will not be used or recorded; this is a completely anonymous survey. You do not need to participate in the survey, but your participation is valuable and appreciated. Even if you do not participate, I would be very grateful if you will forward this email anyway.

I am in debt for your kindness,

Fatemeh Fakhraie"

APPENDIX D

FIGURES OF IRANIAN *HIJAB* STYLES

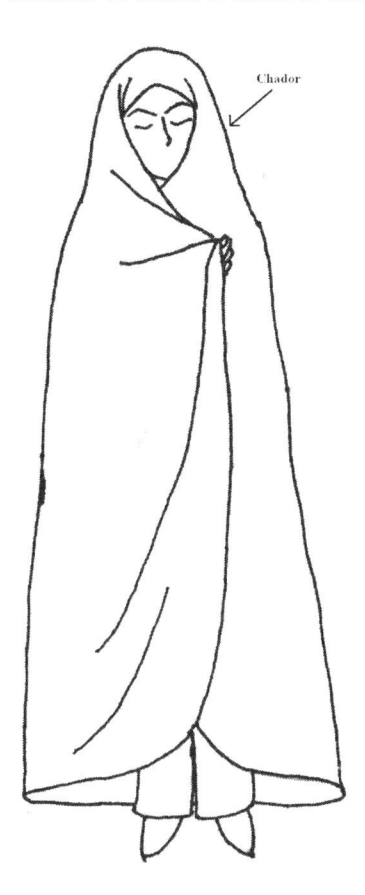

Figure 1. Chador.

Figure 2. Maghnaeh and manto.

Figure 3. Roosari and manto.

VDM publishing house ltd.

Scientific Publishing House
offers
free of charge publication

of current academic research papers, Bachelor´s Theses, Master's Theses, Dissertations or Scientific Monographs

If you have written a thesis which satisfies high content as well as formal demands, and you are interested in a remunerated publication of your work, please send an e-mail with some initial information about yourself and your work to *info@vdm-publishing-house.com*.

Our editorial office will get in touch with you shortly.

VDM Publishing House Ltd.
Meldrum Court 17.
Beau Bassin
Mauritius
www.vdm-publishing-house.com